CRITICAL PATH

How to Review Videogames for a Living

By Dan Amrich

Critical Path: How to Review Videogames for a Living
Copyright ©2012 Dan Amrich

Composed in Palatino and Helevetica Neue Lt Std

ISBN 10:   0-9851437-2-X
ISBN 13: 978-0-9851437-2-5

Printed in the United States of America
First printing February 2012
ROT-10: CVKCR COMBODVOFOV

Images of *Gears of War* used with permission. ©2006, Epic Games, Inc.
Cover image copyright ©2011 iStockphoto.com
Author photo copyright ©2012 Katrin Auch

Copy Editor: Pete Babb
Cover and Interior Design: Katrin Auch
Website: http://criticalpathbook.com

For Katrin, for everything, forever

CONTENTS

Foreword ix

Level 1: What Is It? 1

Pressing Start 2
Five Myths About the Job 4
Coming to Terms 9
It's Not Brain Surgery (But It's Not Nothing, Either) 12
A Tricky Question for the Clever Kid at the Back 16
Whose Opinion Is It Anyway? 19
Critic, Reviewer, Journalist, Other? 22
The Amazing Case of Amazement 25
Here's What Sucks About Your Dream Job 28

Level 2: Learning It 33

Test Your Might 34
Start Your Career Today! 45
Got Any Bright Ideas? 48
Why "Games" Modifies "Writer" 50
Spelling: Teh Key 2 You're Future 53
Seeing Eye to I 56
Self-Editing and Length 62
How Do I Do This, Anyway? 66
A Sense of Style 73
Those Who Can't Do, Write 81
Active Voice 90
Accountability: The Writing 93
Knowing the Score 97
What About Art? 103

Level 3: Getting It   107

Internment...Um, I Mean, Internships   111
Freelancing: Know Your Role   116
"But I'm Already Perfect!"   124
Know Your Masthead   128
Hello, Please Pay Me to Play Games   138
The Guy Who Talked Himself Out of a Job   149
How Freelancing Works   153
Game Gear   158
From Screen to Screenshot   162
Hit Them with Your Best Shots   166
How to Get Free Games   189
Public Relations, Personal Relationships   196
A Tale of Twitter Terror   212

Level 4: Keeping It   219

Welcome to Happy Hell   220
They Promote Editors, Don't They?   230
Writing Not-Reviews   233
Represent!   243
Pros at Cons   249
Going On the Record   253
Accountability II: The Editing   262
The Inevitable Cry of BIAS!   265
Readers and How to Tame Them   267
"How Much Is Your Opinion?"   271

Level 5: Saving It   277

Freebies, Tchotchkes, and "Playola"   278
Where Have I Read That Before?   284
The Care and Feeding of Your Ego   287

Factoring In Your Favorites 291

How It All Falls Apart—and Why That Might Be Good 294

Game Over. Now What? 298

Level 6: 100% It   309

Random Instances for XP 310

Recommended Reading 312

Acknowledgements 318

About the Author 320

FOREWORD

I cannot recall the first time I met Dan Amrich. It might have been at a press junket, or at a convention, or at a random Bay Area bar industry mixer. He's one of those videogame industry staples that seem to have always just...been there. Upon reading this book, I've come to the realization that he wasn't just visiting at various events. He was observing. Watching, and absorbing, like a sponge, the ins and outs of a very complex business that some, still to this date, fail to take seriously.

After all, it's just video games, right? Teenaged kids sitting in their parents' basement, shooting each other, drinking corn syrup, and talking smack online. How hard could it be?

Turns out it's extremely complex, layered, and difficult, on both sides of the fence. As a video game developer, I see journalists as marks, as targets to win over. After all, I've won over the leads at our studio; I've won over the various (often cynical) developers at the studio with my ideas – what's one more super experienced, jaded, hardcore journalist?

Upon initially reading Dan's book, I could have titled it *Abandon All Hope, Ye Who Enter Here* because it really seems like a warning, a shot across the bow that says, "If you're going to go this route, be prepared for a lot of work, be prepared for a low salary, be prepared for exhausting trips. Be ready to claw and kick and scream in order to make a name for yourself, and after that, be prepared to be unappreciated in the vast pit of douchebaggery that is the Internet."

We often see them, gaming journalists, at evening parties, after a few cocktails, or through the filters of Alpha Dog types of public relations people. We see them as pawns, as assets, as potential evangelists that can help preach the gospel of our Latest Title to the hungry, eager masses. We seldom see their side of things, the fact that they're in it for one reason.

Then, upon finishing the tome, I realized why they do it. Those guys, those hard to please, jaded bastards that give me hard questions at every bleary-eyed junket. The other alternate title of this book could easily be *For the Love of the Game*. (After all, it's not the journalists that you see driving around in Italian sports cars.)

The next time I'm at a junket and a journalist asks me a difficult question I'll stop for a moment and think about Dan's book and put myself in his or her shoes. The hours. The work. The criticisms. I'll remember why I got into this business to begin with – because the early games I played as a child shook me to my core; the fact that the interactive medium remains the most compelling form of entertainment that humanity has managed to create. When a game works, and truly works, it does something inside of you that no movie, no book, no television show can stir.

At the end of the day, creatives and journalists aren't that different. We're in the business for the same reasons, and we both take our knocks and our dings, and we keep each other honest. It's that system of checks and balances that maintains a standard of quality that ensures that you, the gamer, ultimately win out.

Cliff Bleszinski
Design Director, Epic Games

■LEVEL 1■
What Is It?

You think you know what reviewing games is about, but you don't—or at least, not all of it. That's why we'll start by clarifying what the job is, what it isn't, clearing up misconceptions, and revealing all the insider bits you've never heard before. It's big-picture stuff.

PRESSING START
You gotta start somewhere (wherever you are now is a good spot)

It's your dream job: Playing videogames. Writing about them. Getting paid. Oh. My. God.

Then you think about it. Your name at the top of a post on Joystiq. A little photo next to your current favorite games in *PC Gamer*. A Top 7 list on GamesRadar.com.

It will never happen, right?

Actually, it *can* happen. Honest. It's definitely not easy to get this dream job—it requires a lot of perseverance, plenty of patience, a certain amount of skill, and a fair amount of luck. And of course, whatever natural talent you can bring with you will serve you well. But with the right combination of elements, it can happen.

The main reason most people don't chase this dream is that they simply don't know where to start. They may have discussions about videogames with friends that are as eloquent and succinct and detailed as any given written review. Or maybe they're the star poster on a web forum, but they don't really know how to translate their insight into a published review for other people to read as an authoritative source. And the people who do know how often keep their lips zipped for fear of their own job security.

That's a shame. The next generation has to come from somewhere, and with it come fresh perspectives and original ideas. At the same time, the industry doesn't need more people who want to be game reviewers because they think it's a cakewalk, looking for free handouts, unaware of the responsibilities that they would have to assume.

So, that's what this book does: It will tell you what you need to know and what you need to do to make a run at this career path, for real. It's not a rigid rulebook and I don't have all the answers. It's still going to be difficult to get your shot. But I have mountains of suggestions and methods based on what I did to get in and what I've seen other people do since that will be enormously helpful. I am happy to say that I have enjoyed this dream job since 1993, when I started writing professionally. I worked my way up from freelancer to staff writer to editor at several websites and magazines, gaining a lot of specialized knowledge along the way. It's knowledge I am eager to share to help you find your own career path.

We'll go from nothing but the desire to write about videogames up through how to get your big break, how to manage yourself once you get it, and what to do once you've been there a while. We're talking press start to game over.

Okay, then. Press start.

FIVE MYTHS ABOUT THE JOB

Where dreams and assumptions are swapped for truth and understanding

There are a handful of popular misconceptions about being a game reviewer—when the job gets boiled down to "I play games for a living," it's easy to understand why. But while it's fun to make other people envious by tossing out that phrase in conversation, it's time to undo some of the damage it's done. When people find out what I do for a living, these are the main questions, comments, and misconceptions that pop up.

So you sit around and play games, right?

The. Number. One. Question. And it's understandable, because hey, wouldn't that be freakin' awesome?! But sadly, it's not the truth. In a typical game editor's day, maybe a few hours is devoted to playing software, but much more time is spent calling game companies, attending meetings, editing copy, hosting visitors for product demos, and all that nuts-and-bolts stuff. As a freelance writer, you may have more time devoted to playing software, but you'll also basically never stop writing—you'll constantly be out there hustling to get more reviews published. Freelancing has its own disciplines and challenges, which we'll get into later on. But suffice it to say that the job is not a matter of sitting down with a controller in hand at nine in the morning and putting it down at five at night, eating candy all day long while making prank phone calls and playing with matches on your lunch hour.

You must be, like, rich

You must be, like, kidding. Writing as a profession is generally not a high-paying gig. Sure, Stephen King and Tom Clancy do fine, but they create original adventures that millions of people want to read. You write about someone else's original adventures that most likely a few hundred thousand people will read, max. King and Clancy are authors. You're just a writer.

Furthermore, consider how many people want this job and are willing to do anything to get it—work for peanuts, work for free, work like dogs. That means there's a cheap labor pool and a hell of a lot of competition.

Here's a sad truth about life and work: There's often an inverse relationship between doing what you love and getting the big bucks. (Ask any starving artist.) Sometimes they come together, but more often than not, having a really cool job is its own reward. You'll be able to pay the rent, but you won't be renting a mansion. And for a lot of people, that's okay. But don't come into this profession with dollar signs over your eyes, or you'll be sorely disappointed in short order. For love or money? Love is all you need.

You get every game for free!

You'll get some games free. You will make friends at some companies, and they will send you an extra copy for yourself or some folks on your staff if you ask politely and if they have them to offer (and sometimes, due to budget constraints or company policy, they don't). As a trusted or proven freelancer, you may find yourself on a few product lists and automatically get each new game that comes out direct from the company that produced it. But you will not always get every game you ever wanted just because you write reviews, and it's rude to expect that you would. What you'll really get is insight ahead of time on what you want to preorder—lots of writers do this. If you can write off your purchases on your annual tax form, all the better, but you should expect to crack open that wallet to get what you really want and line up at midnight for the big software and hardware launches just like everybody else. (The main difference, of course, is that you can then write an article about waiting in line. I've done that several times.)

You must be great at games

Some writers are. Some writers are not. (Play me online, and you'll find out I'm in the latter camp, at least compared to most of the people who read what I write.) Some writers are aces in, like, one or two games—kinda like anybody else who owns a console or two. Your skill in games is like a tool, part of a set that you'll need, and I'd argue that it's not even the most important part. Being good at games is not as important at being good at *explaining* games.

Here's a good example. Back when I was an editor at *Flux* magazine in New York City—a young, snotty youth-culture mag that I still really, really miss—we got a letter from a reader who'd found a factual error in the magazine. We'd done a story on the Top 100 Games of All Time. I goofed, writing down the wrong publisher for one of the titles, and it slipped through our rigorous fact-checking process (which, to be honest, was "Dan, is this right?"). Someone spotted the error and wrote in, full of piss and vinegar, saying, "This is inexcusable—you guys obviously have *no* idea what you are doing. You need someone on staff who knows what the hell they are talking about. You need *me*. Enclosed is my résumé."

Now, *Flux* was the kind of magazine that encouraged a bit of obnoxiousness. I looked at Jeff Kitts, the editorial visionary behind *Flux*, and he said, "Hey, what the hell? Let's give him a shot." Then we read his "résumé," and it contained nothing about his writing or editing skills or experience. It was all about what games he'd played. "Beat *Super Punch-Out!!* in three hours." "Finished *Final Fantasy III* in two days." "Have played and mastered every Nintendo Entertainment System game ever released." Jeff laughed, then turned to me and said, "That's great, but can he write?" Since he enclosed no writing samples, the answer was obvious.

Nobody cares if you can save the princess.

You're important because people listen to what you say

Sometimes, and it depends on what people you're talking about. I've gotten emails from people asking why reviewers don't just call a company ahead of time and say, "Hey, this game is bad, this needs to be improved before it's released." Why not be more proactive? Well, by the time we get our grubby little hands on the games, they're often past the point of sweeping changes. Also, we're not being hired to improve the game at hand, but rather to analyze it once it's done, and tell our readers why the game is or is not worth their time, money, and attention. Hopefully, the developers will improve the *next* one as a result of this feedback, but that's really a secondary benefit. (And for the record, game companies often know their flaws ahead of time, through internal play testing and focus groups. They're just kind of hoping you don't notice them because you're having too much fun.)

You may or may not have an impact on how games are created. Sometimes you may be asked to take a look at a game before it's ready for review, to make suggestions on how it came be improved, but this is rare (and there are professional game-development consultants doing that full-time anyway). If you really want that kind of influence over how a game looks, feels, and plays, you will need to acquire skills in game programming, game production, or art. You need to develop games, not just write about them.

However, depending on where your work appears and how much perceived influence you have, you may be seen as a factor in how a game sells. People who are on the fence about a game might read your review and decide to buy or not to buy it based on your opinion. This is no excuse for power-tripping, but it's important to keep in mind as one of your responsibilities: What you write can and does affect both the people who created the game and the people who would buy it. How much effect your words have is a different matter entirely, but they absolutely can contribute.

So there you go—myths exposed. Everything else you've ever heard about game reviewing is therefore true.

COMING TO TERMS
A little lingo to get things started

Before we go any further, it's important that we define some terms that will be used freely throughout this book.

A *freelancer* is a person who is not on the staff of a publication, but instead writes for several outlets as an independent contributor. Freelancers are paid by the article and are often responsible for providing all their own tools—computers, software, game systems, the works. Like all good mercenaries, freelancers are free to seek work wherever they find it, but they also incur all the fees and risks (travel arrangements, self-employment taxes, and no health insurance) that go with it. However, freelancing is your best way to start out in this industry, especially if you have a day job or are a student with full-time responsibilities of any kind. Some publications list freelancers as *contributing editors* or *contributing writers*.

A writer with a permanent gig is a *staff writer* or simply *on staff*. They've gotten a part- or full-time job at a magazine or a website, and they are usually salaried. The publication provides the tools that they need to do their job. They do the same stuff freelancers do, only they do it in an office—write articles, contact companies, attend product demos. If you're a volunteer staff member for a website, you might not be salaried or work in an office, but your duties will be similar.

The student version of a staff member is *intern*. If you're enrolled in college, you can often act as an assistant to the staff of a magazine or website in exchange for college credit, a small bit of money, or sometimes both. You will get to see the inner workings of a big-time publication by managing the mail, taking screenshots, and doing other grunt work. You'll also be able to get professional advice on your writing, you'll usually score some articles for your portfolio, and you'll establish your first contacts in the biz. Some outlets hire interns for full-time staff positions upon graduation if they like what they see; I know of one magazine that hired at least seven of its staffers from its own intern pool. The main thing is that you usually have to be in some form of college to get the gig in the first place.

That leaves the term most people know: *editor*. What's the difference between a staff writer and an editor? Editors need to know more about the mechanics of good copy ("copy" being journalism jargon for "article text"), and they are responsible for helping steer the publication. Most full-time positions at magazines feature "editor" in their title because you need to know more than just how to write a review or two. Editors have to represent the publication at industry events, meet with companies to demo upcoming products, arrange features and interviews, and work with a full-time staff as the core team.

Most importantly, editors actually create the voice of a publication; they dream up and then create the content that defines a magazine or website. They are the ones who haggle with game publishers for exclusive previews, brainstorm cover stories for magazines and front page events for the website, and then make them reality. And, of course, editors read everything that will be published with a critical eye; they are the arbiters of quality, and it's their responsibility to change, fix, or completely rewrite things as they see fit for the good of their outlet. It's a lot of responsibility.

One thing to note: Writers and editors are not the same thing. All editors can write, but not all writers can edit. It's a different skill set, even if it is complementary. We'll get into it more later, along with some more lingo.

IT'S NOT
BRAIN SURGERY
(BUT IT'S NOT NOTHING, EITHER)
You need to care about what you do, even if other people don't

This might come as a surprise, but I have not always been eager or even proud to tell people about my career. Mind you, I absolutely *love* reviewing games, but there's a lot of misunderstanding when I say what I get paid to do. Inevitably, the immediate question I get in response is one of the following:

[confusion] "So...you make the games that the kids play?" [/confusion]

[incredulousness] "So...you sit around and play games for a living?" [/incredulousness] [greed] "Oh, cool! Can you get me free games?" [/greed]

The middle one is the most common (unless they're 14 or under, in which case it's usually the last one). Play, they reason, cannot possibly be work! "They sell videogames in toy stores. You play with toys? Wow...must be a *tough job.*"

Yes, actually, it is. You will not hear me complain about how unreasonably or unfairly hard the job is, because I have always been grateful for my position and my opportunity; I have never taken it for granted. If I really felt that it was not worth the effort, I would have stopped and done something else. But I do want to convince you of one thing: There is, in fact, effort.

I have two standard self-deprecating phrases I use when I try to explain the job, and this is only so that I don't have to engage this often total stranger in a long, drawn-out ideological battle on the value of media criticism or the nature and importance of play in modern society. One is "Yeah, well, I'm in no danger of winning a Pulitzer." Thank you, says me, I am aware that my field of expertise is not as important as many others, and I hereby give up (*but still secretly yearn for*) mainstream accolades. The other one was always "Well, yeah, it's not brain surgery." That's basically a variation on the Pulitzer joke, but I used it more often because it seemed less cynical and sad.

Until One Fateful Day.

Early on, I mentored a young writer; I wasn't even working in games full-time yet, but I was busting my hump as a freelancer for a then-unfathomable online-only review publication. I had been writing almost all the game reviews for this outlet on my own and editing myself as I went; as payment, I got to keep the games I reviewed. But as the site got popular, the work got to be too much and I realized the gaming department needed to double its staff. Enter The Kid, a teenager who knew how to explain his ideas via the written word and was a good gamer as well. He submitted a few reviews, which required minimal tweaking, and started writing things for me weekly. This seemed to validate my brain-surgery theory—see how easy it is? This guy's not trained at all, and he's doing great.

One Fateful Day, he turned in something that was just awful. Maybe he got lucky those first four or five times, maybe someone was helping him edit his stuff before submission, maybe he'd already gotten too comfortable, I don't know—but I couldn't publish it, and I was stunned that he'd fallen so far so fast. I had to tell him, "Okay, I know you're doing this for free and all, and I appreciate the help, but this isn't good enough." And he was not happy, to be honest. But I worked through what I didn't like with him and it turned into a great learning experience for both of us; he went on to write for me for several years.

But after that experience, I immediately revised my brain-surgery joke to a point that I could no longer use it: "Well, it isn't brain surgery...but it's not nothing, either."

Too many people—reviewers, readers, and total strangers—assume that because the subject matter is fun, there is no skill or craft involved. All you do is play the game and you're done! But the people who make the games we review do not play their way to success; they program and design and test and revise their way to success (failure, too). Game reviewers do it the same way, but I'd still argue that what game developers do is more of a Thing That Matters than what reviewers do. They act; we just react. But even that reaction has a standard of excellence worth achieving.

I hope that other people in my position think that what we do is, if not one of the Things That Matter, at least something Vaguely Important to Certain People Out There. (This may invite a long-winded dissertation on why videogames are an important cultural force, just as important as movies and books and TV and all that. I see their point, but I will kindly suggest that AIDS research or education issues are slightly more important than whether or not Mario could beat up Sonic.)

Ultimately, I realized that anything worth doing is worth doing well enough that you'd be proud to tell someone in casual conversation—and you're still going to have to be reasonably good at what you do in order to find success in this career. If you get this job, it's fun work, but you will constantly be proving your worth, one article at a time.

A TRICKY QUESTION FOR THE CLEVER KID AT THE BACK

I know we're just a few pages in, but it's already time for a pop quiz

I know this sounds like one of those horrible questions teachers pose at the beginning of class to stimulate discussion, but stick with me.

Why does someone read a game review?

(Now, let's not always see the same hands.)

Well, says one particularly clever kid at the back of the room, most people read reviews to get information on the new games that are coming out. Generally speaking, what they do with that information is one of a few things:

- They use it to make up their own mind about whether or not they want to buy the game.

- They use it as a form of temporary escapism, a substitute for their own gaming experience during times they can't play games directly. Reading's the next best thing.

- They use it as their own opinion, so if someone asks them about the game, they sound intelligent and informed, even though they've never played it. The review is their cheat sheet.

- They use it to support the opinion they have already formed. (This happens a lot—some people just want to feel like they are "right" for having already bought and enjoyed a game, and only feel validated if someone with a higher profile agrees with their conclusions.)

They're all true for different readers. Really, the bottom line is that the review gives them information that they can use, however they choose to use it. But here's an interesting follow-up question:

Why does someone *write* a game review?

The correct answer is to provide that information, leveraged with the author's experience and a sense of professionalism, to an audience that wants to read it. The best reviews should also incorporate artistic critique that the game's creative team can use and incorporate next time they make a game, but the creators are not actually your main audience. The consumers of the games are.

The secret but wrong answer to "why does someone write a

game review?"—the answer you will never hear someone admit aloud—is to hear yourself talk and prove how clever you are, or how vicious you can be, under the guise of writing an "entertaining" review. Worse, a lot of people who offer that wrong answer don't know they're doing it, but the truth is there in their writing.

Ego comes with the territory (and gets its own segment later on in the book, which will no doubt make it feel even more important). All writers like to hear themselves talk. All writers like to see their book on the shelf or their magazine on the rack or their review on the homepage. And yes, it is fun to be clever, and it's a hell of a lot of fun to clean your claws on a bad game that deserves it. But that can't be your main motivation for doing this. The reader has to come first—always. The reader certainly enjoys the entertainment value of a harsh or funny review, but self-indulgence wears thin quickly. They will like you if you give them what they need; four or five reviews down the road, the reader will suddenly ask themselves, "Hey, who is this person? Their views are a lot like mine, or at least they explain themselves in a way I find enjoyable and understandable." That's the kind of trust you want—you *need*—to make it as a reviewer in the long term. So don't write for yourself. Write for the audience, the consumer with a buying decision and a touch of confusion. You're here to help, not mock.

I bring this up early because it's one of those global mindset things that you should consider before going any further. It's crucial to get your motivations aligned with the expectations of the audience and your potential employers. You're about to undertake some serious and weighty responsibility. Better to accept it now than learn it the hard way later.

WHOSE OPINION IS IT ANYWAY?
This time—and every time—it's personal

I feel strongly that primary purpose of game review is to levy an opinion. That opinion should be informed by experience, but that's actually the core of criticism: Someone making the judgment call and definitively saying whether something is good or bad (and crucially, why). That's what it's all about.

There's always a bit of discussion about objectivity versus subjectivity in game critique—whether you should really react to a game on a personal level or if you're better off remaining somewhat detached and acknowledging other people's opinions in your assessment. Or, as I was once asked, "Why did you give that game a bad score instead of just saying 'Other people might like it'?"

I understand that approach, but I feel reviews are inherently subjective. They are based on your opinion and your knowledge after engaging in a personal interactive experience; there's a lot of you in each one. Every game you review might not have been created with you specifically in mind, but if you don't state an informed opinion, your review is worthless. News stories are objective, but reviews are subjective.

Let's get semantic. The Free Online Dictionary defines subjective as "particular to a given person; personal." Its opposite is objective, meaning "uninfluenced by emotions or personal prejudices." It's often riding shotgun or downright interchangeable with the word "fair." Well, you want your reviews to be fair, don't you? If a game didn't impress you at first, but as you continue to play, it shows you something you didn't expect, you'd change or amend your notes to accommodate the deeper understanding you'd gained. Writing a review based on the first 20 minutes of gameplay and not altering it based on the next three hours would certainly be considered unfair.

But that does not mean subjectivity is inherently unfair. Looking at the definitions, that "personal prejudices" bit makes it sound scary, like you're going to start the next *Need for Speed* review with "I hate driving games, so…." Yes, that's bad. You're kneecapping yourself from the get-go, saying, "I have no business reviewing this genre, but I am going to do so anyway." If that's where you see subjectivity entering into your work, please stop working.

But do you really want your game review "uninfluenced by emotions"? Games are just as capable of inspiring emotional response as any other form of entertainment. The often-cited plot twist to *Final Fantasy III* comes to mind; if you're not shocked by it, you're not paying attention. A crucial play in *Madden NFL* can make you jump out of your seat and stomp around the room hooting like an idiot just as easily as watching a big game on TV. These are emotional responses that ultimately influence your perception of the game on a personal level.

Furthermore, games are inherently personal in ways music, books, film, and other non-interactive media can never be. You're never a spectator in a game; you're not sitting there letting it tell you a story the way a book or film will. You need to participate to get that story conveyed. You're always *involved*. And in most cases, that involvement is not merely physical; you're doing whatever you're doing because you want to know what happens next, you want to see the next level or meet the next character and progress the story. It's actually your emotions—fear in a survival horror game, aggression in a fighting game, excitement in a racing game, empathy in an RPG, or curiosity in an action/platformer—that drive your involvement. Being emotionally involved is a very, very good thing. It's why you play games in the first place. So why should that not be relayed in your work when it's a common experience among all gamers? We're all in this for the escapism, the rush of glory, the feeling of accomplishment. It's possibly the most powerful element of videogames, period, and yet it's often ignored. So, you know, don't do that.

This is an important thing to consider here at the beginning. When you review a game, don't be prejudiced, but do be opinionated. The former is reprehensible and smacks of a predetermined, indefensible agenda; the latter is based on experience with the game and how it made you feel, and it's the expression of that opinion that lies at the core of what you do.

CRITIC, REVIEWER, JOURNALIST, OTHER?
What you are and what you call yourself might be totally different

When asked, I prefer to call myself a game critic or a game reviewer. "Critic" sounds more accurate to me because I do take the criticism part seriously—praising the successes and pointing out the flaws in a respectful manner is, I think, worthwhile to the people who made the game as well as the people who are thinking of buying it. I don't have all the answers, but based on my prior experience and an understanding of what the game's creators were trying to achieve, I can tell you what I thought, honestly and respectfully. Hopefully it will have relevance to your tastes and opinions, or give the creators the kind of independent, removed feedback they can't get from someone closer to the project. Or you can read my stuff and tell me to jump off a bridge because you disagree. People have. Hey, I'm a critic.

A few years back, I fell into the habit of using the term "game journalist" to describe myself in conversation with people who didn't really know what I did. It sounds good, doesn't it? Sounds important, even legitimate. It sounds better than saying "I play games and say whether they're fun or not." But every time I used the phrase "game journalist," I felt increasingly dirty and fake. Even after several years of writing news, features, and interviews, and conceptualizing hundreds of feature stories, I felt like I was pretending to be something I wasn't. I was not sure if I was taking credit for a respected title that I did not actually do the work to earn.

In my mind, journalists research and report on world events, investigate social injustices, or expose political corruption. I play games and say whether they're fun or not.

That's not to say that you should not consider what you do to be important; it serves a purpose, it fills a need, it helps people seeking advice. But game reviewing follows different rules, different procedures, and different ideals than what many people consider journalism. What journalists do is more than what reviewers do— more investigation, more fact-checking, more information gathering. Journalists, ideally, act; reviewers, by nature, react.

These pithy definitions can evolve. Many game reviewers are also game journalists, either by how they review games or what they do in addition to reviewing games. Other reviewers will remain reviewers but get better at it, and thereby serve their focused purpose even better. I think it's fair to say critique is a subset of entertainment journalism, but the bulk of people writing game reviews are not journalists by default. They're critics. And I believe there is absolutely no shame in that distinction.

This is all very much open to debate. But out of respect for both camps, just know that there is a difference between "game criticism" and "game journalism" and accept that you might not belong to both realms. It's your career, of course, and you can follow either path, even hop between the two. Just know which one you're on at any given time. Self-awareness will help you improve your skills, however you choose to apply them.

THE AMAZING CASE OF AMAZEMENT

Be prepared to let your inner child come out and play—a lot

This sounds silly, but you love games, right?

Yes, I'm serious. Just answer.

Well, assuming you said yes at least once...do you love them enough to let them dazzle you?

We live in cynical times. Ours is a media-saturated society full of irony and sarcasm, where everything is shallow, anything popular is inherently uncool, and the loudest voices are often the voices of dissent. The cool kids at the back of the bus are actually driving. It can wear you down. Sometimes, you just want to escape. And games are one of those escapes.

But if games are your escape from cynicism, why be cynical about your escape?

Games are amazing things. Even the ones that don't offer massive visual spectacle or break new technical ground or win tons of awards can be amazing. Any game can offer something that you've never seen before, something that gives you a thrill.

But you have to be open to it. You have to *want* to be amazed. If you go into a new game thinking you know what you're going to get, you will be disappointed with the experience—and you already have a bad habit that you need to break if you're going to seriously pursue this line of work.

This might be easier to show you than tell you, so I'd like you to indulge me in a little experiment.

Go play a game. Then once you get into it, pause it and turn off the display.

Seriously. Turn it off, stare at the blank screen for about 10 or 15 seconds, and focus. Then turn it back on. I promise, the game will be there when you get back. Go.

Okay, anybody who didn't actually turn off the screen for a little while because they're too cool for stuff like this is not helping. You came here to learn something, didn't you? This is an exercise to illustrate a point—two, actually.

First, it's important to realize that game developer starts with that—a blank screen. How they get from that point to a completed compelling entertainment product is *amazing*.

I think that it's often too easy to forget that game programmers literally create something from nothing. Yes, there are APIs and off-the-shelf tool sets and GUIs and sequels and stuff like that, but ultimately those are means to an end, and the beginning is just an offline idea. I think the commitment that it takes to start with a blank screen and create something—and I don't mean something of quality, necessarily, I just mean *something*—is too often overlooked by game critics. These are the new artists, and their canvas of choice won't even stay put on the freakin' easel. What they do is not easy, and a certain amount of respect should be given up front.

If you can do it too, you already understand. Unfortunately, the bulk of game reviewers aren't able to do it—those who can't do, complain. So if you want your reaction to get respect, offer some respect for the original action.

The second point: When you turned the game off, didn't the whole room feel emptier? Whenever I shut down my machine I always feel like I've just euthanized something. And I think it ties back to point #1. The reason you feel that vague sense of loss and void is that you're used to having emotional responses through that window. Someone somewhere created something in that space that affected you, and it lingered a bit, raised your expectations about what that screen can convey. That emotional response to your window of interaction is worth noting and respecting too.

To me, this is more than just giving a game a chance and approaching it with an open mind before you begin reviewing it. That's basic ethics. This is approaching it with…well, an open soul, I guess. This is introducing your inner child to the controller, a part of you that will be ready to celebrate how much the developers got right. Meanwhile, your inner wizened adult can be amazed by how much went wrong, and that's still of great value to your review.

But either way, you have to be emotionally open to what games do that other forms of entertainment do not do. You have to love this art form and its potential while accepting its problems. But you also have to stay ready to be impressed, if not touched or moved. Your feelings toward games matter because games give you feelings right back—fear, empathy, rage, inspiration, anxiety, joy.

Putting those feelings into words is what it's all about.

HERE'S WHAT SUCKS ABOUT YOUR DREAM JOB
Consider this the "tough love" section

Well, we have to get this out of the way now, before it sneaks up on you and you feel all disillusioned.

Low pay

I brought this up before in the part about myths, but you really need to accept this reality going in. Some of your favorite big-name game bloggers are making five bucks (or less!) *per post*. A full-time entry-level position at a major gaming publication might pay 25 or 30 grand a year—and, if you're lucky, include health insurance. Promotions and higher pay will come with persistence and performance, but keep your expectations in check. There are a whole lot of jobs that offer more money for less fun, so some of your biggest compensation in this field will be job satisfaction.

Long hours

Deadlines are a reality, and this is not a 9-to-5 job. Publishing deadlines are notoriously inflexible in print, and the web never sleeps. You will work late and on weekends to hit your deadlines, even as a freelancer. This may mean canceling plans with friends (or not making them too far in advance), jeopardizing any romantic relationships you may have, and missing out on key moments of your life. Be prepared.

Your audience is jealous

Everybody thinks they can do it better than you. Get ready for over-analysis from unpublished Internet trolls who criticize everything you write, and sometimes, the stuff you haven't written yet but surely will fail at writing correctly in the future. The truth? Maybe they *can* do it better than you—but often the loudest voices are the ones with the least ambition. The people who really want to show that they can do it better are busy honing their chops just like you. This doesn't mean you should discount criticism from your audience, but you should consider what might be driving it.

Your audience is going to yell at you

It's not rational, it's not normal, but it's inevitable: Sooner or later, business becomes personal, and a simple matter of opinion will be presented as a matter of life or death. For instance, if you give a game a 9 and someone out there thinks it should have gotten a 10, you will receive the verbal equivalent of a shotgun blast to the face because you "hated" the game. (This exact thing happened with *GamePro*'s *Metroid Prime* review.) In a case like that, the reader didn't see any flaws, but you did, so you're the idiot. It's good to be accountable for what you write, to be available to discuss it with the people who read it, but sometimes it will turn ugly.

There will be no parade in your honor

As I've already mentioned, a lot of people won't understand or respect your area of expertise, no matter how good you may be at it. It's a little like debating the merits of mild cheddar versus extra sharp cheddar with a person who is allergic to cheese.

So...that's the truth. You'll be poor, you'll be tired, you'll be under a lot of stress, and you'll be hated by gamers and non-gamers alike.

Welcome to your new career!

LEVEL 1 WHAT IS IT?

■LEVEL 2■

Learning It

Now we get into the nitty-gritty of writing, everything from grammar and tone of voice to pre-made mistakes that you can easily avoid. We'll also discuss what you can do right now to kick off your career, even if you don't have a job.

TEST YOUR MIGHT
Think you're ready? Let's find out with this sample review

One good way to show what to do is to show what not to do. Here's a sample review for a fake game; it's about 300 words, which is a common review length for many outlets. I'm using a fake game so that you can read it like your intended audience—assume they've never heard of this game before, they've missed all the previews, and have yet to see a single screenshot. They stumbled upon your article with no preconceptions or knowledge of this game. The review should tell a newbie everything they need to know. And today, you are that newbie!

Yes, this review is loaded with intentional mistakes. Unfortunately, I've seen similar articles submitted by freelancers as final copy, and I've seen their editors weep. There are five major mistakes made in the text below; your job is to find them and think of how you would fix them before I reveal the answers on the following pages. Happy hunting.

LEVEL 2 LEARNING IT

Alien Shot
Developer: Interstellar Studios
Publisher: Firestorm

Alien Shot is the newest game from Intersteller and it is par for
the course for the developer. You play a space marine sent to
a base on an alien planet where something has gone wrong.
The cool thing is that the aliens have the ability to take human
technology and upgrade it, so you will find new weapons
never before seen by humans. Throughout the game you will
get to use them all in a variety of ways and slaughter waves of
enemies in interesting ways.

The graphics are pretty standard for a game like this—
detailed textures of slimy alien corridors give the game a good
atmosphere. The camera doesn't cause too much trouble, but
occasionally it gets annoying. The blood effects are pretty cool,
even if the aliens bleed green.

Control-wise, the game is as solid as you could hope for. The
left analog stick is used for moving around the base, and the
right analog stick aims. Trigger buttons are used for shooting
and grenades, which is comfortable. Aurally, the explosions
sound good, and the character dialogue is, too, especially in
the cutscenes that move the story along. The opening cinema
features a track by Palette-Swap Ninja, one of Starco Records'
hottest bands.

The main problem with the game is that it feels like we've all
played this game before. While it's fun to shoot aliens and
the new weapons are cool, the basic gameplay isn't anything

special. It's pretty undemanding, but it's solid nonetheless.

Overall, *Alien Shot* is not a bad game for the money. It would make a good rental for the weekend if you have nothing else to play, especially with the multiplayer options. Overall I give *Alien Shot* a 7 (out of 10).
—Alan Smithee

Did you spot the areas that need improvement? Let's take it piece by piece:

Alien Shot is the newest game from Intersteller and it is par for the course for the developer.

Hey, look—all five problems are right here in the first sentence!

1. This is a horrible lead. The *lead* (sometimes spelled *lede*) is the first sentence or paragraph in a review (or any article, for that matter), and it sets the tone for what's to come later. More importantly, it's your only chance to grab a reader like our target audience, the one that doesn't know anything about the title or have any emotional investment in it yet. Why should they read your review? The lead gives them a reason.

Writing a good lead is not easy; it takes effort and practice, and you won't always get it right. But you should work at it until you come up with something engaging here, because if you don't give the reader something compelling, they will turn the page. While this lead seems to get down to business, it is not engaging.

2. The use of passive voice makes this whole review boring to read, and that usage starts here. Sometimes, the verb "is" is appropriate

for use, like in the sentence you're reading right now. But passive verbs like "is," "are," and "does" kill all the energy in a review and don't pack a lot of power. "*Alien Shot* is the newest game from Interstellar" would be more compelling as "Interstellar's newest title *Alien Shot* promises…" (or "lacks," or "offers," or any other active verb that fits your opinion). We'll get into active and passive voice later, but the appearance of "is" twice in a sentence, let alone the lead, is a major mistake.

3. "Interstellar" is misspelled. Maybe the game studio spells it with an "er" at the end to be cute, or maybe the studio follows the dictionary with an "ar" spelling. Dunno—the author used one spelling in the header information and another in the body text, so either could be correct, and at least one is definitely wrong. Your spell-check program will not catch this, so you must check this fact manually.

4. The game is described as "par for the course for the developer." What course is that? What other games has Interstellar created that make this seem like it's an expected release for the developer—do they specialize in alien action games, or mediocre games that could be better with some more effort, or something else? The reader has no other information to go on at this point, so if you can't explain it succinctly in the lead, you need to bring this up later, after the article and its feel have been introduced.

5. It's not a major issue, but the phrasing of "for the course for the developer" is repetitive. Sometimes you will have to use this sort of "galloping" structure to string a bunch of prepositional phrases together, but not often. Here, it's not a huge sin, but avoid butting these up against each other when you can; always look for a way to

rephrase your statement. (In this case, the real culprit is the cliché "par for the course," so eliminating that would help.)

You play a space marine sent to a base on an alien planet where something has gone wrong.

6. Maybe the plot of the game is generic, but your description of the plot does not have to be. The "alien planet where something has gone wrong" is about as vague as you can get. Surely there's something even a little bit more detailed that could be added here to tell the reader where and under what circumstances the game's action takes place?

The cool thing is that the aliens have the ability to take human technology and upgrade it, so you will find new weapons never before seen by humans. Throughout the game you will get to use them all in a variety of ways and slaughter waves of enemies in interesting ways.

7. From a quick glance, it feels like the weapon selection could be the game's most interesting element, the one thing that might set it apart from other space action games. Weapons can be upgraded, or have been upgraded, or something like that—but the reader needs a specific example here. Have the rocket launchers been converted to shoot symbiote eggs? Or can you combine a machine gun with an alien device to simply make a more accurate machine gun? These new weapons are not only "never before seen," they're never fully explained, either, so the reader cannot share whatever excitement you felt when you first discovered them. Same goes for the "interesting ways" in which you can dispatch enemies; without a specific example, it carries no weight.

8. How do I hate repetition? Let me count the "ways." There are two of them. That's hardly a variety of ways, and definitely not interesting. Simply reading your final draft out loud will help avoid repetition problems like this one.

The graphics are pretty standard for a game like this—detailed textures of slimy alien corridors give the game a good atmosphere. The camera doesn't cause too much trouble, but occasionally it gets annoying. The blood effects are pretty cool, even if the aliens bleed green.

9. Once again, the author saw something specific in the graphics and made a comparison to other games—but once again failed to explain what they were or identify the basis for comparison. Vague words like "standard" and "good atmosphere" don't paint a mental picture. Even "detailed textures"—an overused, abused, nearly empty phrase—says very little. Better to talk about what kind of atmosphere the graphics create.

10. The line about the camera poses the same problem as the above; it's too vague to be helpful, plus it says the camera is both a good thing and a bad thing at the same time. But this phrase also poses another twist that you might not have seen coming: There's a camera in the game. What kind of game is this? Is this an isometric view action game, a third-person action/adventure, or a first-person shooter? You could have started reading with any of those assumptions, and you'd have a good chance of being right. The article never specified, and it should have.

11. The aliens shouldn't bleed green? Seems like a valid creative decision that the team made; why bring it up? If the review author

disagrees and feels the enemies should bleed a different color, it would be appropriate to say why green isn't the best choice, or what they felt would work better and why. Does green blend in with the alien skin textures, or maybe the environment backgrounds (are we fighting aliens on a lush jungle planet)? Or is this purely a value judgment that human blood is red, so red blood is "realistic" and therefore somehow better? There are two paths here: More substantiation for the argument or the removal of the comment altogether, since it seems to have little bearing on anything else. Who knows what the author's intent was, but as it is, it reads like "This game isn't gory enough."

Control-wise, the game is as solid as you could hope for. The left analog stick is used for moving around the base, and the right analog stick aims. Trigger buttons are used for shooting and grenades, which is comfortable.

12. "Solid controls" goes into the Vague Cliché Hall of Fame. It's honestly tough to describe what makes controls successful—it's part ergonomics, part programming, part black magic. That's the curse of a good control scheme: If you feel connected with the game and you're unaware of the controls themselves, they're excellent...and invisible. If they're bad, of course, it's easy to dedicate a paragraph to what's wrong and why (too many buttons in a combination, sluggish analog response, etc.). Still, "solid" doesn't really tell you anything beyond "the controls work." Better to suggest a move you might perform in the game and mention how easy it was to perform and why.

13. Any time you read a review where the author describes how the controls are assigned, drop it and run screaming. The player will

learn this information as soon as they crack open the instruction manual or, more likely, the moment they pick up the controller. Noting which function is assigned to which button is totally worthless, and it proves that the author is not thinking critically about the game's controls. Mentioning that the trigger-triggered grenades are "comfortable" is a step in the right direction; it's as if the author was trying to pull this one out of the fire. But it would be much better to describe one of the game's firefights and illustrate the control mechanics through that.

Aurally, the explosions sound good, and the character dialogue is, too, especially in the cutscenes that move the story along. The opening cinema features a song by Palette-Swap Ninja, one of Starco Records' hottest bands.

14. "Aurally" is rather awkward. A lot of times, writers run out of ways to introduce the element of the game they are discussing—they want to address the graphics as one issue, they want to address the sound as one issue (and some publications have templates that specifically request that you comment overtly on those elements individually), but they don't want to fall into the trap of saying "The graphics are…" and "The sound is…" with all those nasty passive verbs. It's a noble goal, but it often falls flat as they start reaching for the thesaurus for other words that mean "in terms of the sound." It's easy to grab a synonym that doesn't quite fit the context of the game or the writer's own style. And that's what happened here.

15. Why is there an ad for Starco here? That doesn't help the reader; that helps the record company. Name-check the artist if they made that opening cinema more interesting or noteworthy, but the record label mention reeks of copying from a press release.

The main problem with the game is that it feels like we've all played this game before. While it's fun to shoot aliens and the new weapons are cool, the basic gameplay isn't anything special. It's pretty undemanding but it's solid nonetheless.

16. The good news is that this is an actual critique, identifying a large issue with the general feel of what it's like to play the game. The bad news is that it's so vague it's not helpful to the reader. If the gameplay feels familiar, it's okay to name names; if it seems to draw inspiration from specific titles that came before it, mention them. If you played them, your reader might have, too.

17. Here's another chance to describe exactly what makes the weapons cool, and the author dodged it a second time. We know how the reviewer feels, but we still don't understand exactly why.

18. "It's pretty undemanding, but it's solid nonetheless" is an empty, contradictory phrase. Mixing a slightly negative word like "undemanding" with a slightly positive word like "solid" doesn't give the reader anything beyond a feeling that the author is wishy-washy and either unable or unwilling to take a stand. Some games are mediocre and don't inspire strong feelings, but your writing should never follow that lead.

Overall, *Alien Shot* is not a bad game for the money. It would make a good rental for the weekend if you have nothing else to play, especially with the multiplayer options.

19. If the reader had anything else to play, they would likely not be seeking information on a new game. How often have you said to yourself, "Well, I have this game that I'm really looking forward

to playing this weekend…but maybe I'll go rent something else instead." It's a silly thing to suggest. When you want to predict gamer behavior, think about your own.

20. Wait, there are multiplayer options? We're 280 words in and heading toward the final sentence; this should have come up earlier. Of course, since the rest of the review is so vague, we don't know what that multiplayer experience might entail. Is it cooperative play, or do the aliens square off against the space marines? What kind of gameplay options are introduced or change? Some games offer great multiplayer but lousy single-player, or vice versa. Don't sweep it under the rug; for many people, multiplayer is the big draw and the key to replayability.

Overall I give *Alien Shot* **a 7 (out of 10).**

21. The author just used "overall" at the top of the paragraph in an attempt to wrap up the review with a summary. Here it is again. Watch for word repetition. Also, make sure you don't repeat yourself.

22. If you're working with a rating scale, the rating will get its own box on the page. There is no need for you to waste words on it—not only is it redundant, but sadly, some readers will skip straight to the number score anyway and ignore the rest of the text!

23. This game seems to have nothing to recommend it, nothing to make it stand out from the crowd. From the text, it's really just a mediocre action game—middle of the road. So why does it rate a 7 instead of a 5, which really would be the middle of a zero to 10 ratings scale? The author needs to make sure the text supports the score and vice versa. Editors will often call writers on this mismatch

and ask them to pick the one they really meant and amend the review so that the text and the score are consistent. Other times, editors will just change the score because by the time you've turned in a review, it's really their property now.

24. By the end, what did the writer actually tell you about their experience with the game? Not very much. They went down a checklist of things that they thought they had to mention— graphics, controls, sound—but they never actually imparted a feeling of what it was like to play the game. (If the graphics and sound don't define the game experience, you might not even need to mention them.) When a friend asks me about a new game, it's always one simple question: "How is it?" And if your review is not answering the question in an emotionally satisfying way—if I don't feel that you felt anything, even apathy—then your review is not getting the job done.

If you found five mistakes, that's good. If you found more, all the better—you're already looking at copy critically, and that's crucial. You'll have to start looking at your own writing as well as other people's writing this way.

START YOUR CAREER TODAY!

No job? No problem. Don't let a lack of employment keep you from the rest of your life.

It's easy to get caught up in the Catch-22 of the game review biz. "I haven't reviewed any games because I don't work at a publication," I hear you cry, "but nobody will hire me because I'm not published."

So don't wait for them. Do it yourself. Do it now.

You may have seen those cheesy "Start your career today!" ads on TV. Well, writing game reviews independently really does give you the freedom to start your career today. You already own a machine that plays games, whether it be a portable handheld system, a laptop or desktop computer, or a dedicated console that flickers images in glorious high definition. That's pretty much all you need to get started (though that laptop or desktop computer would help, too, just for the whole typing thing). Play a game, formulate an opinion, and write it down. Everything after those three steps is pure refinement, so you might as well practice now, while you have the time.

Starting a career doesn't necessarily mean having a job. Building the skills, gaining the knowledge, getting experience... it's all relevant, and it's there for the taking whether someone is necessarily paying you to do it on their behalf or not. So until that day arrives, do it yourself, following similar guidelines and rules to what you'll be expected to follow when you are on assignment. This book will give you the insight and info you need to know how to write for that magical day, but it's worth sharing your goal someone else—a teacher, a parent, a writer friend—and working with them to improve your skills. You can gain experience now, and then turn it into a profitable career later.

While you're woodshedding, you may also want or need to acquire some skills that have nothing to do with your prowess with a game controller; they're more about your ability to convey your ideas to the rest of the world. For instance, do you type? Full and proper speed-freak touch-typing isn't a necessity, but typing in some form—even if it's the weird "advanced hunt-and-peck" lobster-claw finger-smashing I've seen some of my colleagues employ—is a must. As a writer, your keyboard is your best friend. And hey, there are games out there to teach you typing. Some of them are actually fun. But it takes time. And since you don't have a job in the biz yet, well, take that time and do what needs doing now.

YourReviews.com?

You can create your own game-review website in about 10 minutes (thanks, WordPress!). But is that something you *should* do? Sure, why not—it will give you an excuse to start writing and have a place to store your work publicly. If you come up with a particularly insightful editorial or a killer review, you will easily be able to share it with friends, family, and yes, potential employers.

Keep two things in mind, though. One, despite the fact that anybody can type in your domain name as easily as the URL for a major site, your one-person blog is not going to compete with sites like Kotaku, Joystiq, and Destructoid. Hopes, dreams, and aspirations should not be replaced by delusions of grandeur or unrealistic expectations about getting mobbed by traffic. Think about how many gaming websites already exist and just how hard it will be to have your voice heard among all that noise. They all have a head start, probably by several years. If you are able to earn and retain a small, loyal audience this way—say, one or two hundred regular readers—you'll be far ahead of most amateur game writers.

Two, doing this all yourself or perhaps with a few friends who share your desire to do this "for real" means you are not working with a professional editor. If your copy is naturally strong enough (a big *if*, to be fair), then you might be able to use the clips on your homegrown site to solicit freelance work. But editors will often want to see some evidence that you will be receptive to feedback, can follow their rules, and won't throw a tantrum when your work is edited. We'll get into this more later, but simply saying "I started my own site" is not necessarily the feather in your cap you might think it will be. Saying "I contributed to this small but already established site" is better in the long run.

If you do set up your own site, it's more beneficial to think of it as a dojo, or maybe a science lab. This is where you practice and experiment, where you learn new techniques and play with form and structure, where you can create the articles that help you find your voice and personal style. If the thrill of writing in the semi-public eye helps motivate you, then it's absolutely worth setting up your own site. Just don't convince yourself that the hard part is then done.

GOT ANY BRIGHT IDEAS?
Don't forget to be creative— and please do it on command

Some people assume that creativity is something that just happens. Nope. The "thing that just happens" is inspiration; creativity is how you personally apply it. When people say "come up with a creative solution to that problem" or "think outside the box," this is what they mean. Do something I haven't seen before. Find the unfamiliar within the familiar.

This is a key concept because you need to think this way at every stage of your writing, from the headline you create to the word choice of your review to the critical points you make within it to the very structure of your review itself. Is there a more entertaining way to present this idea? Are you answering the questions your audience is likely to ask? Are you adding something to the discussion with your point of view, or are you just repeating yourself or others? Creativity means constantly pushing yourself;

creativity is pleasantly surprising people with how you say what you say. And as a writer, how you say what you say defines you to both your readers and your employers. What's more, you'll often need to say these creative things on a deadline and within a structure—a review template, a word count, an embargo, things like that. You need to be able to make something interesting from nothing at all on command.

There are many ways to nurture your creativity, all of which are personal. I don't mean to cop out here, but telling you what kind of music I listen to when I write or that I get a lot of good ideas in the shower doesn't help if you don't listen to music or shower. The more you write, the more you will find these methods naturally. By constantly varying your approach to your writing, you will learn what methods fire off the right sections of your right brain. But once you have found methods that work, start using them and start refining them, as you will need them for the rest of your life.

As you progress, there's an easy way to tell whether you are hitting the creative mark or not. When you read a game review, you go in with expectations. There's going to be discussion of the game's various elements and how well they worked (or didn't work) and why. But it's what you get that you *don't* expect that makes the work memorable; it's when the information is presented in a more entertaining, more insightful, more succinct, more interesting way than you bargained for that you really internalize what you've read.

Games themselves are not boring; they're challenging and innovative and are praised when they offer something unexpected within the context of the comfortable. Your writing should be doing exactly the same thing. That's creativity.

WHY "GAMES" MODIFIES "WRITER"
Writing about games is great, but it's not enough

I get a lot of letters asking for advice on what classes to take in school for a career writing about games. "I am going to school specifically to learn how to write about videogames," they say. "What do you suggest?"

I suggest you not do that. Instead, go to school to learn to write, period. Locking yourself into one genre of writing—just reviewing videogames—is bad for all sorts of reasons, but one of the final ones is that you may find yourself unable to do anything else. Expand your focus; this branch of writing is too young and can only benefit from a broader perspective.

An old, simple saying is also very true: "A writer writes." That is, if you are truly dedicated to being a good writer and not just a games writer, the fact that you get to write about videogames is a luxurious, cherished bonus. You should be able to write on any topic (and *want* to write on other topics—you do have other interests, don't you?) using the same set of skills. My college classes included everything from obviously applicable things like personal essay and persuasive argument to less evident but extremely helpful courses on humor and business writing. By the time I got to focus on critique, it covered books, movies, television, theater, music, and art. I had to do them all, often in real time—taking notes in a dark movie theater, reading a book by a deadline, trying to understand a painter's intention and statement and then turning my interpretation into something compelling and coherent on its own. It was difficult. It was good. It was the perspective I needed.

I always encourage aspiring writers to write as much as they can, for practice or for publication, because that's the only way you'll improve. There is no substitute for experience when you are trying to find your voice as a games writer, but I also think more value needs to be placed on the breadth of that experience. Absorb multiple influences and generate articles on multiple topics; you may be amazed to see how your skills develop and cross-pollinate. It's for your personal benefit as well as the media's. We need more writers who cover games and less gamers who think writing is a pretty cool job.

And Why "Games" Should Modify "Reader" Too

For quality output, you need quality input. As you're writing, you should be reading—not just gaming websites, but any printed form of journalism, from CNN.com news reports to a preview of a new car in *Motor Trend* to the entertainment supplement in your Sunday newspaper. For instance, pick up a copy of *O*, Oprah Winfrey's magazine. I promise it will not hurt you. I also promise that their interview features will feel different from what you see in the gaming world. Maybe you will find you like their technique and want to try it yourself.

By casting a wider net, you will see what other editors have already approved as worthy copy for a major publication, and you will see stories written in completely new contexts. All of that exposure will help you grow, and you will slowly absorb it as you create your own voice.

The more you read, the better you'll write.

SPELLING: TEH KEY 2 YOU'RE FUTURE

Drop the online acronyms and ditch the txt msg shortcuts; it's time to spell like an adult

Before you even consider seeking work as a game reviewer—or any writing profession, for that matter—you absolutely have to know your spelling and grammar, inside and out. Some people are probably rolling their eyes as they read that, thinking they are too creative to be bound by the restrictions of English, but guess what? You're not. And what's more, you're asking for acceptance and employment from a community that really believes in it.

Every time you read a review in a professional magazine, it has gone through several editors, each of whom has checked the article not only for clarity, but for spelling and grammar errors as well. Every magazine also features at least one copy editor, whose primary role is to check spelling and grammar, along with style things like whether it's "deathmatch" or "death match" and whether you should spell id's series of shooters "*DOOM*" (the way id wants it) or *"Doom"* (the way most publications actually choose to do it). The copy editor is there to make sure that what gets published is of the highest quality and follows all the rules of the English language.

When it comes to tech realms, bad communication habits are easy to acquire. Shortening words to single letters may help when you're sending text messages and might not pose a problem in a chat room, but it's not acceptable in any other realm. If you want to work in this industry, you must know how to spell.

Grammar is generally trickier, and some publications adopt a relaxed policy—that is, they want the magazine or website to reflect the way the readers actually speak, the way "normal people talk." That's fine, but keep in mind that you're always expected to know the rules before you are allowed to break them.

For years, one of my catchphrases has been "Welcome to life. Spelling counts." Mistakes happen, but a responsible writer recognizes them and finds out how to correct them. It is not a sin or a shame to open the dictionary (or even easier, look it up on a dictionary website). You are not expected to know everything. You are simply expected to know *how to learn* everything.

Here's the harsh truth: As an editor, if I see a spelling error in your cover letter or résumé, chances are I'm not reading any further. Colloquial grammar, sure, I can let that go. But I'm looking for someone who knows how to express themselves accurately and is at least smart enough to put their best foot forward. If you can't be bothered to double-check for errors on something as personally important as a job application, I'm not going to risk finding out if you will be bothered to check an article for errors before it goes out to half a million readers. And even today, I don't rely solely on computer spell-checkers for my work; they help, but I find reading my articles aloud helps me identify issues quickly.

Of all the tools of the trade, your writing skills are the most basic and therefore the most important. If spelling and grammar aren't priorities to you, they need to become priorities immediately.

Look It Up

Good research habits are no less important than spelling and grammar. Over the course of writing articles, you are going to need to find raw information—titles with proper spelling and punctuation, release dates, developer backgrounds, quotations, you name it. That does not mean that you look on Wikipedia and assume it's true; it doesn't mean you ask Twitter. This means actually ferreting out the information by doing your own research.

It's not that hard. Do you know how to use Google? You're halfway there—get to it. Of course, it depends on where Google takes you as to whether or not you can trust it—make sure your source is credible and *their* facts are right. Publisher websites are best for titles; retailer websites are often useful (though not entirely accurate) for release dates if you don't see one on the publisher's site. Developer websites often have the entire company history noted on an About page. And of course, there's always picking up the phone and asking the company in question, just to be safe. "I just want to make sure I'm accurate" is a call they will always gladly take.

Also, don't be that person who asks a co-worker every time they need a factoid. Don't expect them to stop what they are doing to find out information for you; that's not research, and believe me, nobody likes that guy.

SEEING EYE TO I
Using first-person voice in your reviews
can be extremely effective...or deadly.
Which will it be for you?

Another pop quiz: What's one letter than can instantly skew and ruin an otherwise good review?

"I."

This is something of a hot-button issue. Use of first person in reviews is always a tough call; it used to be forbidden, but styles have changed lately to incorporate it. *Entertainment Weekly* lets its movie reviewers use it. Magazines like *Game Informer* regularly use "I" and "we." Many news blogs embrace first-person voice.

The main question is this: Does first-person language in a review bring the reader closer or keep them further away?

The use of first person is understandable and shouldn't be considered *verboten*; it just needs to be used wisely and for the right reasons. Whereas books and movies put you on the sidelines as a spectator, nothing happens in a videogame without your input. Every game is a personalized experience for each player—you move, you choose, you shoot, you drive. It makes sense to use "I" because the entire experience is a personal one, and, well, you're the one *doing* everything. To wit, you can't spell "interactive" unless you start with "I."

In a publication context, it's cool to tell the reader, "Hey, we're just like you," and the word "we" can certainly do that—like, say, "we can't wait for this game to come out," or "once we got our hands on the beta, there was much bickering about who got to write this preview." When used correctly and carefully, "we" can be extremely powerful and inclusive and really make the reader feel like they belong. This technique is often called "the royal we."

Like anything with power, the word "I" must be used responsibly. Often, your subjective opinion has to represent a larger entity; writing for free for your own website is one thing, but writing for a pro site or magazine made up of a dozen or more staff members complicates things. It's your name on the byline, but people will say "the magazine gave it a good review."

That's still a good case for "we," actually—"we give it a 7 of 10." Authority, community, speaking as one unified entity to the audience—those are rational reasons to want to use first person. But that's all for the plural "we." The singular "I" is far less easy to justify, though it does have its place.

For instance, I reviewed the 1996 PC puzzle game *Endorfun*, which supposedly sent you positive subliminal messages (stuff like "I love the world and the world loves me") buried in its New Age soundtrack while you played. The game was overtly trying to make a personal connection with each and every player and *change* them. (Every game is trying to make a personal connection with the player, but very few are trying to change its players as *people* outside of the game.) So I made a joke about that, suggesting that it had altered me and my perceptions. It was short, but it was there, and I did use the "I" in that instance, parroting back some of the messages the game was telling me (they were listed in the instruction manual), saying something along the lines of "I think *Endorfun* is enjoyable, and I must be right, because according to the game, I am a genius." It had a clear context there, but I haven't felt the need to use "I" in a review much, if at all, since.

Some of the folks rallying around the first-person flag sound off base, as if they're looking for a way to justify their egos. Your reviews should be based on experience, past and present, and they should be *your* opinion, but while your ownership of that opinion may be paramount to you as a writer, it's not paramount to the reader. You are not the story.

Sometimes the push for first person comes from an egotistical place—lazy writers who think they themselves are the reason a review is read. Nope. Game reviewers are not rock stars. You can be as charming and as charismatic as you want, but it does not make you more important than anybody else, especially the reader. If you're lucky, people might recognize your name and look forward to seeing your next article, but that's because of your last article, and the article before that. They're responding to your work, not to you. Ego is never a legitimate reason to choose first-person voice.

A review is read because the reader wants to know about the game. That review is then worth reading because of your experience and analysis. And at the bottom of that food chain is you yourself, merely the delivery boy for your opinion, which is really just a framework for information about the game.

They're buying the game. They want your review's information. They kinda don't care about you.

The worst mutation of this that springs to mind came from the well-respected magazine *Next Generation*, which was essentially a U.S. version of the legendary British games magazine *Edge*. I loved *Next Gen*. It was a great leap for the legitimacy of videogame magazines, one of the first I remember reading that seemed to give its audience credit as adults. And while it didn't use the personal pronoun "I", the magazine's style was to use phrases like "we here at *Next Generation* look forward to this game with interest." Hmm. That's not the same "we" of shared affiliation or belonging; that's the royal "we" in a bad, weirdly exclusionary way.

What's more, whenever the words "Next Generation" appeared in an article, they were bolded. Okay, that's just pompous, and maybe that was the point, but that's the very heart of thinking that you are more important than the material you present. Use of a standard "I" or "we" would have been far less distracting.

Ultimately, the print version of *Next Generation* never found a mass appeal audience—which may not have been its goal, but I'd argue that part of the reason for the mag's limited success was this exclusionary tone of voice. It made the reader feel like they were lucky to be allowed to purchase a copy. It's a shame that's part of the magazine's legacy, because its actual content was top-notch, and its interviews with important industry professionals were the best in the biz. (*Next Generation* morphed into *Edge*'s daily game industry news website, www.next-gen.biz, which I recommend. I don't notice the "we" thing in its current incarnation.)

If you're writing for an existing publication, ask about their style when it comes to first-person voice. If you are writing for your own independent outlet or one that does not have a style rule, then ask yourself why you want to use it. If it's for egotistical reasons, re-evaluate. If you honestly feel first-person voice will make the readers feel affiliated and welcomed, then use it wisely and keep the fine line in mind.

New Games Journalism

British game critic Kieron Gillen popularized the phrase "New Games Journalism," or NGJ, in 2004, and it struck a nerve with a lot of gamers who'd grown up on cookie-cutter previews and reviews. His alternate approach was more than just using the first person; it was also about sharing personal experiences and anecdotes to frame the observations and opinions about the game in question. It doesn't read like a traditional review or preview; it's more of a personal essay and shares more with travel journalism or "new journalism" (mixing literary fiction elements with reporting — Tom Wolfe coined the term in a book by the same name in 1973) than the gaming coverage that has traditionally appeared in enthusiast magazines. The most oft-cited example of NGJ is "Bow, Nigger," by Always Black, which explains the gameplay of *Jedi Outcast* while also offering terrifying insight into unfounded racial biases in online games. Read it at alwaysblack.com, in the blackbox section. It's brilliant.

New Games Journalism may have been a reaction to the heavily templated review system that came before it, but it's not a replacement (and, it should be noted, it's not always suggested to serve that purpose). NGJ is heavy on opinion and impression but very light on the purchasing advice and strict evaluation that many gamers turn to game magazines and websites to get, so if a reader comes seeking that advice, all they'll get is disappointment. What's more, if the writer isn't disciplined, it's easy for a NGJ evaluation to slip into a self-indulgent ramble that has little relevance to the reader, or even the game itself. Yes, I'm sure that was a tasty stack of pancakes, but does referencing what you had for breakfast and how cool your friends are really help anybody know how to spend $60?

I think that games writing has now learned the lessons of New Journalism from the 1970s; feature stories in particular are already written experientially, describing gameplay and visits to developer studios or recapping events with personal editorializing. As a result, I think NGJ can be (and has been) integrated into "old" games journalism to make it more relevant and engaging in the modern world. When I first read some of the NGJ examples, it looked to me like someone was writing an op-ed column without the column. I suppose it's all about context, and in that context, it looks less like a revolution and more like quality creative writing.

If you haven't tried writing in a more personal style, it's definitely worth a go. You may find you have something valid and valuable to say when you color outside the lines, but I'd suggest you only experiment once you learn how to color within them.

As a rule of thumb—especially when you're trying to get work from a media outlet—don't confuse an essay with a review. While both are valid, social commentary and software critique are often different things, and you should respect your audience's need for one or the other.

SELF-EDITING AND LENGTH

What you don't say can speak volumes.
It's also easier to read.

Most writers start out eager to talk about everything they experience. That's fine; in fact, that's to be encouraged, because articles without substantial info suck, and you can't offer detail without using words and specific examples. But at the same time, while you want to go into detail, it's not required to go into *every* detail. Some people write long reviews out of sheer enthusiasm; others just don't know when to shut up. It's all too true that some writers like to hear themselves ramble on and assume that readers are hanging on their every word. You need to divorce yourself from what you write or you'll lose your perspective on the subject and therefore your review's usefulness.

Case in point: In the early, wild, lawless days of online publishing, there was a gaming area on AOL that featured no screenshots but tons of text—I remember reviews offering 2000 words on *Wipeout* for the PlayStation and 1600 words on *Killer Instinct* for the SNES. (By contrast, most print reviews then and now average between 300 and 500 words; in the modern era, even Joystiq's *Gears of War 3* review just barely topped 1200 words, and most of their reviews are shorter than that.) Friends told me they loved that site's reviews because they went into so much detail and didn't treat the reader like an idiot. But after a little exploration, it became clear that few of my friends actually *read* the entire reviews. When pressed, some of the site's most outspoken fans admitted that they skipped to the end and read the "bottom line" section. That encapsulated summary usually ran a whopping 100 words. So that's what they really found useful—a short, efficient "is it good or is it bad" opinion—and the rest was considered fluff. It was a perfect illustration of what the writer wanted conflicting with what the reader actually needed.

Where your work appears will have great bearing on how long it should be, but here's a good rule of thumb: It should never take longer for a person to read your review than it would for them to pick up a controller and come to their own conclusions. Your review acts as a shortcut to personal experience; hopefully the reader will get their own experience in time, but until they do, what you say should tell them what they need to know about a game.

To that end, learning to edit your own work as you go is truly one of the best things you can do. First and foremost, there's the question of creative control. If you turn in copy that needs to be edited, someone else will edit it—and they may unintentionally change your meaning, skip a detail, or remove a part you'd consider too important to remove.

Mind you, some parts will have to be removed. Everybody gets edited, and it's best to view it as a positive process. Sure, there are style preferences and creative differences, but first and foremost, word counts are unavoidable. In print magazines, only so many letters fit on a page, and they're not chopping down an extra tree just so you can ramble on about the game's backstory. Websites have no inherent space restrictions, but some choose a maximum number of words for reasons of clarity, reader usefulness, and screen layout. So don't take a word reduction as a bad thing. Shorter, tighter, more efficient prose is better.

Furthermore, editing your own work makes you more valuable to editors because they know your writing will be clean and tight when it comes in, which makes their job easier (and you more employable). And—no surprise here—learning to clean up your own work is the first step toward the job security of cleaning up the work of other people as a full-time editor.

So how do you do it? Working with someone who knows more than you is key. Find a teacher, a family member, or a friend with a knack for words and have them look at your writing. Write a sample review, then ask them to edit it. They will identify problems and places for improvement, and you'll be able to address them. The more you do this, the more obvious (and easy to fix) those elements become, and the more likely you are to correct them as you go.

And sometimes all you need is a sounding board. I rarely write anything without reading it out loud, preferably to my wife, Katrin, but if she's not around, I simply read it as if I were reciting it from a podium or on a podcast. The parts that are awkward or repetitive leap right out at me because I have trouble saying them aloud. Other times, I hear myself say something and realize that it isn't really what I wanted to say, or I find I've left out a key word of a sentence. Just one spoken run-through usually turns up two or three things that can be immediately and easily improved.

Self-editing is a process that you'll have to explore at your own pace, and the more you write, the better you'll get. In time, you'll find that your writing becomes clearer and cleaner from the start, and you won't even realize you're editing yourself; it becomes internalized, and you do it on the fly as part of your regular writing process.

Making self-editing part of your regular writing routine is a big, crucial step toward being able to do this at the professional level.

HOW DO I DO THIS, ANYWAY?

A five-step process of turning random observations and snarky asides into something actually useful

Writing a review is a multi-step process. If you don't already have a method that works for you (every writer is different, so every process can be different too), try this, which is how I generally approach a review.

Step 1: Game on

Play the game and take notes as you go. Write down everything that pops into your head, because you never know what observations will wind up supporting your opinion when it's fully formed. This step doesn't have to be fancy or structured—keep a pad of paper nearby and pause often, or go straight to your word processor and type in the phrases that leap to mind about control, replay value, graphics, sound, and your overall enjoyment as you play. (At home,

I have my computer desk 180 degrees from my console gaming setup: I swivel between the two screens while I play and take notes.) You may be surprised to find that your first instinct is often the best instinct: Your early detailed notes will often turn into sentence fragments for your finished product. Nobody will see this stuff but you, but make sure you write down complete thoughts because nothing's worse than reading your notes three days later and wondering, "What the hell does that mean?"

Step 2: Outline and first draft
Write your first draft. Make it as long as you like—write everything you want to write, so long as you keep a coherent structure and it follows whatever template it's supposed to follow. The sooner you do this after the notes, the better, as the game details should be fresh in your mind. You do not have to have a final score in mind at this point; it should be suggested by your text anyway. Try writing a quick outline of the points you want to cover; many writers find that this helps them stay focused on the points that matter most as they flesh out their ideas.

Step 3: Walk away
Leave it for a day, or at least overnight. Give both the game and your opinion time to sink in. Have a burrito.

Step 4: Polish
Give your work a final edit. Find out the word count and pare down the text until it fits. Identify the parts that support your main thrust and prioritize them; start looking at the stuff that might be interesting but doesn't actually prove your primary point. That's the stuff to cut. This will hurt, because you will have killed off jokes or observations that you are very proud to have written, but honestly,

they don't matter as much as the stuff that supports your argument. When you're done, it should be spot-on to the word count and as tight as you can make it.

Step 5: Save everything

Save both the rough version and the edited version in different files. Sometimes an editor will come back and say, "Can you lengthen this by 200 words? We had another review drop out, and we need to fill space." It's better to be prepared, and it's also a good idea to compare the two versions to see just how much (or how little) changed beyond the word count.

If you find a different method that works better for you, by all means, use it. But this one ain't bad.

HOW DO I
NOT DO THIS?
If you don't make yourself aware of these painful mistakes now, you'll keep on making them forever

In every writer's search for a balance between information and entertainment, they wind up making mistakes. Part of the learning process, sure, but if you're going to make mistakes, at least make original ones. Here are a handful of fundamental major errors to avoid. Look for them in your own work and be ready to rewrite.

Genre cluelessness

Ever read a role-playing game review by someone who has clearly never played a role-playing game? It's painful. Their experience is light, so their insights are equally shallow. If you want to review a game in a specific genre, go find out what you need to know (ask friends, rent games) before you start levying critique. The worst kind of review is an uninformed one.

Platform bias

"I hate Game Boy games, so...." Amazingly, that's the first line of several reviews I've read, and it never ceases to disgust me. Why are you reviewing the hardware? This is a software review. Never mistake your biases (including your preferences) for a particular gadget or console for your opinions about the games it runs and the experiences they offer. A lead sentence like that instantly invalidates everything that follows it.

In-jokes with nobody

You and your friends may think that quoting dialogue from an obscure horror film or dropping in song lyrics from a killer indie band's seminal album is great fun over dinner, but nobody's laughing outside of your inner circle. Remember that tastes and cultural awarenesses vary wildly, and showing off how cool you are by the entertainment you cite in a review is a recipe for hipster disaster. I've had to cut clever references that I personally loved but simply didn't believe the audience at large would understand. Your references must be relevant to your audience. You can bet that gamers know Shigeru Miyamoto, Lara Croft, and Master Chief. You can bet they probably won't know Django Reinhardt, Michael Moschen, or Tom Lehrer—and even if they do, those people probably don't have any direct relevance to the game, so why mention them? No reason, other than to flatter yourself, so don't do it. (If you happen to be writing for a publication that also covers obscure horror movies and indie music, well, don't listen to me.)

Plain ol' arrogance

Some reviews express an alarming overconfidence that stems from...nothing really, other than the desire of the author to be seen as an expert. It's largely in the tone of voice, which can suggest inflexibility, arrogance, or superiority; specific word choice and sentence structure can factor in heavily, too. Look closely: Are you judging more than just the game you're reviewing? Well, maybe you don't know everything. If you've lost your objectivity on your own writing, a friend can help read your copy and decide if you're veering into haughtiness.

Parroting instruction manuals and tutorial levels

I see this one a lot in new writers who have run out of things to say in their review, but feel compelled to fill it up with words, like a fifth-grade book report. A review is supposed to be an informed opinion, not a recitation of the booklet that comes with the game. So when you want to explain how the game's mechanics work or what the controls feel like, make sure you're not saying anything the controller diagram can already tell you. The fact that the B button fires is not inherently interesting or useful to know unless using the B button to fire is a uniquely effective, novel, or disastrous way of making the on-screen weapon fire. (And if that's the case, explain it in decent detail.) By extension, a list of every button assignment is just pointless, especially to a reader who's wondering if they should play it at all. Don't tell them what every knob and lever in the car does; let them know how it feels to drive.

"Facts"

Not sure how a character's name is spelled? Check the publisher or developer's website. Want to mention when the game came out? Surely your local store can tell you. Still feel the need to discuss the actual button functionality? *Now* it's time to crack open that instruction booklet, because you never want your reader to read your work and shout "Idiot! That's wrong!" It's easy to goof on spelling, or a developer's history, or any one of dozens of other small supporting points that can strengthen your review's authoritative tone...but only if you get them right. Stupidest lazy mistake I've seen: A preview that incorrectly identified the platform on which the game was running. Seriously.

Limp scores

I find it a little sad that the text of a review can be so easily ignored, but for a vast majority, it's the score that matters. Whether you're giving a game a letter grade, a set number of stars, or a number between 1 and 100, make sure that your text and score match. Beware not to judge a game as mediocre and then give it 7 out of 10. Um, wouldn't that be a 5? Likewise, every game you review isn't going to be the Best Game Ever. You start giving out 10s like they're candy, and suddenly everybody will get sick of your candy, not to mention suspicious. Make your scores mean something, and support them directly with as many concrete examples as possible when you write your text.

These mistakes can befall any writer of any experience; the difference is now you know what to look for. And don't worry, there are many more out there. Believe me, you'll find them on your own. I still am.

A SENSE OF STYLE

There are a lot of ways to write something wrong. That's where a style guide comes in.

Pop quiz: Is the popular mode of online play spelled "deathmatch" or "death match?" Does Pac-Man spell his name with a hyphen or without? Should game names be italicized? And are you writing about "video games" or "videogames?" If you've never even thought about that stuff, now's the time to start. The answers to those questions, in order: It depends, with, it depends, and it depends.

Nearly every professional publication has a style guide because nearly every professional publication has its own spelling and grammar preferences. For instance, *Official Xbox Magazine* italicizes game names, whereas *GamePro* did not. But each of these publications keeps a list of terms and spellings and other nitty-gritty rules as their editors express preferences and debate word usage, and that's how style guides are born. With the exception of the correct presentation of brand names like PlayStation (capital S, always) and Xbox (not XBox, X-Box, or x-box), a style guide is little more than an organized list of The Way Things Should Be Said

According To Us. Some magazines and websites will offer their style guide to freelancers or potential freelancers if you ask (and we'll cover that in another chapter) but chances are, if you're starting out from scratch, you won't have a copy of anybody's style guide before you start writing your reviews.

Thankfully, there are a few reference sources out there to help you make some of these often arbitrary calls.

The Associated Press Stylebook
The Chicago Manual of Style

AP and *Chicago* are arguably the two biggest influences over published style. Many publications refer to one or the other for the bulk of their choices—things like which words should be italicized; how, when, and where job titles should be capitalized; variations on punctuation; how to write numbers (is it "ten" or "10"?); and other down-and-dirty decisions. Which one is better is always up for debate as both cover similar ground. The paperback *AP Stylebook* is thinner and more affordable than the hardcover *Chicago*, with a focus on specific terms and an easy alphabetical structure. It's easy to navigate, but it's not as thorough as it could be (but maybe just as thorough as most people ever really need). *Chicago* started covering technology word and phrase usage with its 15th edition, offers twice the pages of *AP*, and goes into much more detail concerning citations, punctuation, and other hardcore writing rules. It's a little tricky to navigate, but it's also available as a subscription website, which covers both the 15th and 16th editions. You can sign up for a free trial at http://www.chicagomanualofstyle.org.

Here's the funny part: When I asked around to find out which magazines preferred which stylebook, I consistently got the same type of answer: "mostly *Chicago*," "*AP* style, with some exceptions," "heavily modified *Chicago*," and so on. In other words, *AP* and

Chicago set the standard, but then it all gets customized anyway when editors start thinking about what looks comfortable or "flows better on the page." One managing editor told me that while he was familiar with both *AP* and *Chicago*, his magazine officially used neither.

This sort of "we respect the rules but don't necessarily follow them" approach is born out of a desire to keep things conversational. Editors want their gaming publications to be friendly, to speak to the reader as "one of them" and not be a detached academic tome or a stern judge that hands down scores and opinions from on high. Games are fun; the text should be fun, too. And that often means incorporating slang terms or colloquial phrases that gamers will understand. There's a good chance that *AP* and *Chicago* will not address terms like "pixel shader" or "pwnz."

However, that doesn't mean *AP* and *Chicago* aren't worth having on hand, especially when you consider that you will need to know the rules before you can decide which ones you choose to follow. If you're serious about this career, make the $50ish investment to put both on your bookshelf for reference.

For the sake of it, I looked up "video games" and "videogames" in each manual. *AP* says the term is "video games" as two words in all instances. *Chicago*'s 15ᵗʰ edition doesn't specify either way, but an article on *Chicago*'s website about italicizing game names suggests they support two words...even though "videocassette" is one.

The International Game Journalists Association Style Guide

A whole bunch of people who have been writing about games professionally and semi-professionally have already given the "video games vs. videogames" question plenty of thought. David Thomas, Kyle Orland, and Scott Steinberg codified everything in the *The Videogame Style Guide and Reference Manual*, making this as a good guide to follow as any—especially considering the price. It's a free download in PDF form from www.videogamestyleguide. com, or you can order printed softcover or hardcover editions for reasonable prices. And from the title, they clearly believe there is no space in "videogames." Take that, *AP!*

Wired Style

The hippest, most engaging publication on all things digital created its own style guide too; along with dropping the hyphen from "email," they suggest a lot of other rules for newly coined terms in an interactive world. It's out of print, but finding a used copy should be easy enough. It's well-organized and unpretentious. Also, *Wired Style* says the term is "videogames"—"one concept, one word."

The dictionary

As with *AP* and *Chicago*, many publications pick a specific edition and defer to it in times of indecision or debate. For some, it's the latest version of *American Heritage*; for others, it's *Webster's*—and then you have to decide if you're talking the Collegiate version or the standard edition. Still others like the granddaddy of word books, the *Oxford English Dictionary*. Again, there's no wrong answer here; for what it's worth, *Merriam-Webster's Collegiate Dictionary, 11th Edition* has been the choice at several places I've worked. Just don't be afraid to crack that bad boy open from time to time. You can also use dictionary.com and m-w.com for quick reference.

Your favorite gaming magazine or website

You have one, no doubt. Just start paying attention to what they do, or read through some back issues/archived online articles to find examples of some of the more specific phrases, even if it's just the handful discussed here. The more experience you have as a reader of the publication, the more likely you are to already know (and maybe have already internalized) these stylistic choices. The more different outlets you read, the quicker these little choices will jump out at you.

Your personal style guide

It's not crazy to make your own style guide, based on what you learn from all of the above, because honestly, this is what your favorite magazine or website does. This is not as hard as it sounds; it's as simple as keeping a list of terms on your computer that feel comfortable and "right" to you when you see them. Then, make sure you are consistent in your usage; don't write it "videogames" some days and "video games" other days. Pick one style and stick with it.

It wouldn't hurt to spend an hour or so searching the Internet for "style guide" and seeing what turns up. You can often locate specialized style guides for all kinds of writing—legal documents, HTML, and research papers (the guidelines set up by the Modern Language Associations, or MLA, is a popular one for those) all have their own house rules. They're worth browsing, especially if you're still looking for what form a style guide takes.

Even without a style guide, you should know the grammar basics that your teachers tried desperately to cram into your head back in grade school. That's the cornerstone of your writing ability. You know the trouble spots: "all right" versus "alright," "your" and "you're," and of course, the most difficult three-letter combination in the English language, the dreaded distinction between "its" and "it's." These are three examples of hundreds, if not thousands, of ways to make mistakes in your writing. You absolutely will need to know the core grammar rules at a high school level, without exception. Because with any luck, neither hundreds nor thousands but *hundreds of thousands* of people will read what you write.

Much of the style guide considerations are situational; you

won't know the publication's specific rules until you're already elbow-deep in writing assignments, so don't think you have to start memorizing esoterica just yet. However, you're already better off knowing they exist and preparing yourself to work with them.

Oh, and enough teasing: Is it "video games" or "videogames?" The old guard of *AP* and *Chicago* seems to think it's two words, and the new guard feels it's one. Since the new guard writes about games more often, I choose to side with them. Personally, I play videogames.

HEADLINETK

There are some stylistic choices that are unique to the world of publishing that you'll never hear anywhere else—this is stuff you only find out from working at a publication. But if you know them starting out, you already speak part of the secret language of the pros.

Proofreader's marks

Not many publications use proofreader's marks any more, as most edit teams revise things digitally, but there exists an entire sub-language of squiggles, slashes, and abbreviations that used to be the working language of print publications. If you would like to look into the past, you'll find a list of the most common marks in the *AP* and *Chicago* style manuals as well as some of the larger dictionaries, but you will likely never use them in your work. It's more important to learn how to use Track Changes in Microsoft Word.

One space after a period

In the typewriter era of monospaced fonts, two spaces after a period was the standard. That era is long over, and computer fonts handle the proportional spacing just fine for you with just one space following a period. Yet some folks still believe that two spaces at the end of a sentence is the correct way to write, and some of those folks may be your parents or teachers. Your parents and teachers are wrong. One space is the preferred form. If they doubt me, ask a typographer.

TK

Some people write for years without seeing this term, and it's fair to say it's somewhat archaic, but once you start using it, you never seem to switch gears. TK is an abbreviation that means "to come"—writers insert the letters TK (preferably capitalized) in place of any information they don't have at their fingertips but don't want to stop and look up while they're in their creative groove. Usually the TK information is something easily fact-checked, like the proper title of a person being quoted, a product's retail price, or the number of levels in a game.

There are a few obvious questions about TK: If it's short for "to come," why not "TC"? Because that's too close to "TOC," which stands for Table of Contents. Why bother typing PRICETK or TITLETK or 19TK instead of something simple like "XXXX"? Well, some people do use X for the unknown stuff, but there aren't too many words in English where T and K appear next to each other, whereas plenty of gaming words use the letter X, even in multiple—Vin Diesel's action movie *XXX* featured a game tie-in, for instance. TK is so obviously different and awkward that it jumps off the page and is easy to spot when you're doing a final check of your work. And in case you're wondering, you should avoid typing something long and obvious like "IWILLLOOKTHISUP" in the space because there is nothing more embarrassing than seeing the long and obvious phrase "IWILLLOOKTHISUP" show up in the final product. At least if TK slips past the final edit, it can be written off by the audience as a typo, not a glaring factual error. And you don't want to be the person who writes a long tirade about missing information instead of a simple "TK," because that tirade might look enough like real content to get printed, and you will be embarrassed when it does. Yes, it has happened.

-30- or

Now we're talking really old-school. Writing is one of those professions steeped in tradition, mostly from the newspaper world, from which all other forms of entertainment writing arguably have blossomed. Typing "-30-" or "###" on its own line at the conclusion of a manuscript was the signal that there was no more copy and no further pages. Some writers still use it, but they are generally part of the old guard who started out by submitting a stack of papers to their editor. The advent of word processors (with end-of-file markers, scroll bars, and cut-and-paste functions) makes this more or less unnecessary, but some writers still like to use it out of a sense of tradition.

THOSE WHO CAN'T DO, WRITE

Before you pass judgment, pass one of these simple game-development tests

You are unlikely to find a music critic who has not, at some point in their lives, played a musical instrument or tried to sing. Similarly, most movie reviewers have more than just a love of watching films; chances are high that they've tried to make one, either as a student or by penning a screenplay. Book reviewers? Many have an old draft of a story that they've written that they can't bring themselves to throw away, assuming they're not actively working on the next Great American Novel between review gigs. Hell, some of them have already written the Great American Novel. John Updike wrote for *The New York Review of Books* for several decades when he wasn't winning multiple Pulitzers for his own work. Talk about a tough critic.

Now ask your average videogame critic how many games they've helped create. Betcha it's a pathetically low number, like zero.

Studying the art form with intellectual detachment is all well and good. It's even necessary, to remain informed yet objective. You need a wide, deep pool of examples on which to base your opinions. A book reviewer must be able to cite multiple books with good plots and others with bad ones to know the difference. And certainly, nobody wants to read a movie review by a critic who has only seen *Citizen Kane*, *Pretty Woman*, and *Team America: World Police* before they fire up their word processor and start doling out advice to other people.

And yet, that's the current standard for videogame critique. All you have to have is experience playing games and a command of the English language to be considered qualified in the role of critic. That's not only shameful, that's crazy!

The old saying is true: There is no substitute for experience. Until you have tried (and quite probably failed) to create a game, you cannot truly appreciate the effort involved—especially because that is effort that you may deem not good enough with a low score. Ethically and responsibly, you have no right to pass judgment if you can't say you've done it yourself. You need to do the work of a game developer if you're going to tell them how they should do their job.

This doesn't mean you have to go to college for computer science with a minor in fine literature just to be able to say that the story of *Alien Shot* is almost as weak as its graphical effects. There are lots of ways you can try to create something in videogames pretty much immediately.

Interactive fiction

Before there were graphics, there was gameplay. In the late 1970s and early 1980s, folks like Scott Adams and a team of writer/ programmers at Infocom helped pioneer the field of interactive fiction (IF), a computer-based narrative story that unfolded based on what the player typed in. Simple two-word commands like OPEN

DOOR and TAKE PISTOL and ZAP ALIEN led to florid, clever prose worthy of any hardcover novel, except that the story progression changed based on what commands were typed in. Games like *Zork*, *Planetfall*, and *Deadline* riffed on medieval fantasy, sci-fi, and murder mysteries respectively, while other titles took on tricky stuff like romance and comedy. An author of no less stature than Douglas Adams was a fan; he helped Infocom create the official interactive version of *The Hitchhiker's Guide to the Galaxy*, which is still a fiendish classic of the text adventure genre. As an encore, he wrote an original Infocom game, *Bureaucracy*.

Interactive fiction is a perfect way for you to try your hand at game design and programming all at once. Come up with a concept—a post-apocalyptic tale of survival; a treasure hunt that takes place in your local mall; the hilarious misadventures of a priest, a nun, and a rabbi in the afterlife—then make a simple 10-room adventure game. You'll need to plan out the story, map out the world, describe all the surroundings, determine what the player can and cannot interact with, choose how they can interact with them, suggest why they would want to interact with them, write responses to any way they might *think* to interact with it, determine how the objects interact with the environment, figure out how the objects might interact with each other, structure the puzzles, make them solvable, and keep score. Easy!

The tools to create interactive fiction are free, and you have multiple options for languages in which to write your game. There are also some great tutorials online. When you're done, you can run your game on anything from a PC to an iPhone and many other unlikely devices. (I've seen some text adventures that run on scientific calculators.) It'll also be teeny-weeny and can be emailed to all your friends as an attachment. That's the beauty of a text-based game with an open source code.

Seton Hall professor Dennis Jerz provides a fantastic interaction-fiction primer on his website; point your browser to http://jerz.setonhill.edu/if/ and get started.

Add-ons and mods

You don't have to create your own game from scratch. Making a new part of an existing game is valid. Pick a PC game you know and love—*The Sims, StarCraft II, Grand Theft Auto IV, Quake III, Minecraft*, whatever. If it's a hit, other people are into it, too, and they're looking to expand and extend their gameplay experience. The key to that is the modification community, which exists to do exactly that—remix and enhance games that were already good to begin with and make them better, or at least different. *Counter-Strike*, for example, went from a homemade mod for the original *Half-Life* to an official Internet religion.

At any given time there are hundreds of mod teams working on upgrades, improvements, add-ons, or total conversions for dozens of popular games, and you can help. Make a new weapon model for *Skyrim*. Create a custom piece of art to hang on the wall of a Sim household. Turn *Half-Life 2* into a steampunk epic. Design custom fatigues for *Counter-Strike: Source*. Build your own *Portal 2* death chambers. You will need to learn how your game of choice was put together, but many games ship with an entire suite of content-creation tools tucked away on the installer disc. They're specifically supplied so that users can dig in and make their own content. To the game's creators, that's the ultimate compliment.

If you and your friends don't want to start a new mod and if you don't want to join a team of strangers, there are things you can do solo, like making new textures ("skins") to replace the clothing/armor/look of a game's existing player models. When *Quake II* came out, I made a large handful of skins that resembled the *GamePro* editors, so we would know who we were shooting on sight in our office games. It was a lot of work, but they were good enough to release to the Internet (just barely!), and I learned some advanced Photoshop tricks in the process. All I needed was information on how *Quake II* needed that texture file to be laid out and what colors I was allowed to use, and I was off and running. All that information was available in *Quake II*'s thriving mod community.

Start poking around the fan sites of your favorite game and see what interests you, then download the tools and get involved.

Game-developer-in-a-box thingies

There are oodles of people who love games and have a great idea for a game but have absolutely, positively no hope in hell of programming one themselves. Whether it's a lack of time, patience, or math skills, they know that their ideas are going to stay locked up. But what if a PC program could do all the hard bits, leaving you to decide things like what the enemies should look like and how many points you get for shooting down an alien mothership? Now you're talking.

Despite its age, The Games Factory 2 from Clickteam is still a popular program for creating 2D platform and shooter games; if you want to try to make the next *Sonic* or *Galaga*, try it with The Games Factory. If you want to take a crack at making an old-school, *Zelda*-style role-playing game, look for the RPG Maker series, which not only lives on PC, but even had a PlayStation edition. Game Maker is regularly updated and has a strong support base, and for 3D games, try—what else?—The 3D Gamemaker. These are not the only options; there are similar products out there to help you make your ideas into working prototypes, if not actual shareware. Some of these programs might cost you a little money, but the ones that aren't free are priced at about what you'd pay for a new game. It's all about what you want to create and how deep you want to go.

XNA

Download Microsoft's XNA C# programming tools (they're free) and make your mini-masterpiece, then run it on PC or Xbox 360 (the latter requires a fee). With a growing field of indie developers using XNA, you won't be alone; the community is full of strong supporters helping each other learn the tools and create their games. Any existing C programming skill you may have is fairly easily leveraged.

Mind you, any one of these paths is still going to be an isolated, small-scale exercise that nobody else may ever play. But the point is, it's worth a try. Try to do this yourself before you go out there and tell other people how it should be done. If you can create your own *Tetris* clone, more power to you. If you can't, there's nothing wrong with failing. In fact, it's recommended—failing at making your own game will show you just how hard it is to do it right.

When you sit down to write a review, a bad game is still going to be a bad game, no matter what your personal creation turns out to be. Knowing that it takes a long time to make a high-quality texture is not an excuse for releasing a game with a crappy one. But knowing firsthand what some of the challenges those developers faced makes their failure a little more noble and makes you a little wiser. You will at least understand what they were trying to do because you tried to do it too. You still have to tell readers what is worth their money and what is not, but you should be doing that from a position of experience not only as a writer, but as an amateur game developer as well. And you really have no excuse not to try being one.

FROM START TO...HMM
Anybody can pick up a controller to start forming an opinion, but when should you put it down?

When a music critic reviews a CD, they wouldn't dream of skipping a track. Every minute of that disc is listened to and evaluated, not to mention the liner notes.

For movies, Roger Ebert doesn't fast forward through the screener copies he gets. He watches the whole film from the start, possibly multiple times, and makes up his mind after careful consideration of everything he's seen.

And if you're going to review a book, it's not like you can just skip to the end, find out the butler did it, and levy an opinion. That's a good 10 hours of reading, usually.

And with videogames...um. Yeah. Videogames have the potential to be 10 times longer than books. Some action games might be between 6 and 10 hours; that's a fair estimate for a skilled player zipping through to the end. But some games take longer—let's say about 25 hours if you're digging through the whole single-player campaign and checking out what multiplayer has to offer. A deep RPG like *Skyrim*? Estimates can easily hit 150 to 200 hours, as can an entire season played out in a sports game. And let's not even bring up online RPGs with foreboding names like *EverQuest*.

So what's the ethical line here? If only based on the amount of time it takes to play all the way through, can you reasonably be expected to finish a game before reviewing it?

The answer is yes, whenever possible.

The "whenever possible" part is clearly the stickler here. As a freelancer, you are expected to have more time than a full-time staff writer or editor, and therefore you can do it the right way the first time. But the reality is that I've written too many reviews without finishing the whole game due to time constraints and having to juggle multiple projects at the same time. It's something I'm not proud of, frankly, but it was part of the situation I was in for several years. Never enough time, and no cessation of deadlines.

Waah, waah—tell that sad "situational ethics" tale to the developers who put a minimum of 18 months of their lives on hold while they sweat over a hot debug trying to tell a good story. Is it fair to them? Hell no. If you want games to be thought of as art, then you've got to extend them the necessary respect to go with it. You don't review an album by listening to the single, and you don't review a book by reading the first few chapters. Play the damn game.

Now, there are some games that you can't finish. Go ahead— beat *Tetris*. Collect every car in any given *Gran Turismo* game on a deadline. And let everybody know what's at the end of *World of Warcraft* while you're at it. In those cases, it's more about the time invested, both quality and quantity. You have to trust your own instincts to know that you've seen enough of the game to levy a useful and, above all, fair critique. And sometimes, a game's poor design or relentless difficulty may stop you from finishing the game, but that is a rarity. When it happens, that needs to inform your review, if not act as its entire basis.

Be honest with your editor about whether you've finished the game before you've reviewed it. They will need to defend your review, and they can only defend it fairly if you're being fair with them in turn.

Reviewing a game is a time investment. But like most investments, the time you spend before coming to a conclusion will pay off.

ACTIVE VOICE
Here is the single best thing you can do to improve your writing right away

You're a gamer. You've used cheat codes. There aren't many cheats when it comes to writing reviews, but here's the next best thing: One trick that will instantly improve your writing and give you a much better chance of being taken seriously as you set out into the wild and lawless world of game reviewing. And the best part is, it's not a trick at all—it's just a basic element of good, energetic writing.

There are two kinds of verbs: Active and passive. Passive verbs are verbs like…well, like the word "are." Is, are, was, were…they describe a state of being. *The traffic light is green. We are going to meet up later. Sonic is really fast.* Passive verbs just sit there. They get the job done but without passion.

Active verbs positively *bleed* passion. Active verbs add color and energy to your work and, more often than not, tighten up the prose, resulting in a stronger, more efficient read. And just to hammer the point home, active verbs populate the entirety of this paragraph.

Ask any English teacher, and they'll remind you that the big difference is how the subject of the sentence behaves. If the subject is being acted upon, you'll see a passive verb: *The meeting is taking place later.* The meeting looks like it happens without your involvement. But if the subject is acting, they'll act with an active verb: *We'll meet later.* Whoa—suddenly you're in charge. Videogames give the player control; videogame reviews should take the same approach.

Let's put this into a review context. Here's something you might read in any game review:

While the soundtrack is energetic, it doesn't seem to match the theme of the game, which is medieval.

That's a mixed bag—it starts passive with "is," goes active with "match," then fizzles out with another "is." My trick here is to turn these passive statements into adjectival phrases. If the soundtrack is energetic, call it an energetic soundtrack. Do that and your resulting sentence sounds a lot better:

The energetic soundtrack feels like a poor match with the medieval theme of the game.

By tweaking the "doesn't seem to" phrase to be "feels," we've tapped into how the game is an emotional experience (which all good games should be, and which is what you need to strive to convey in every review, even if the one you're discussing is not), but also made the statement sound more authoritative. What's more, using the phrase "seems to" pulls punches, like you're not really sure if you want to make that call. But it's your opinion—go ahead! As long as you can explain it, say it: "This feels awkward."

Just one problem, though: As the sentence stands, it implies that the game does not deserve an energetic soundtrack just because its theme is medieval. Those separate points are not related in the critique. One more tweak should do it.

The soundtrack, while energetic, matches poorly with the game's medieval theme.

There ya go.

There are some places in your writing when passive voice is absolutely the right choice. Sometimes a passive verb preserves clarity. If you are writing a news story about a videogame company, for instance, passive voice helps convey a "just the facts" approach without making it seem like the author is getting in the way of the material. However, videogame review offers no such restrictions. You always want to aim for the intangible "feel" in your reviews— that's what you want to try to express, and nothing expresses feelings better than active verbs.

Videogames are inherently exciting and engaging. (Um, I mean, "By design, videogames excite and engage.") Your writing should match—and your writing will be memorable for it.

ACCOUNTABILITY: THE WRITING

It's not just what you write...well, actually, it is

The Internet is awesome, especially for gamers. We have tons of websites and hundreds of forums where we can meet and freely exchange our ideas about what we love, hate, and hope for in this hobby. Everybody's out there speaking their mind, which is a beautiful thing...in theory, anyway. In practice, it often devolves into flame wars, insults, wild assumptions presented as fact, and images of babies getting attacked by birds with the legend *PWN3D* Photoshopped over them.

Why do people communicate this way? Because as MonkeyGamer7598, they can get away with saying things that they would never say if they had to say them face to face. When your public name is not your legal name, and your avatar of choice is not your real face but a picture of a *Dragon Ball Z* character known for hitting people, it's much easier to hurl ignorance around. Everyone's anonymous on the Internet; accountability is sadly optional.

The problem, then, is when MonkeyGamer7598 decides to read this book and thinks his special brand of argumentative wit will get him a job in the game-review biz. Even if it's really entertaining, if he's not accustomed to having to back up what he says, he's not going to get far. (But he'll probably complain about how unfair it is in his next forum post.)

Before you get your work into the hands of too many editors and make too many bad first impressions, keep in mind that what passes for communication out in the loose communities of the web does not always pass for legitimate professional communication at your finer media outlets. It very often holds little in common with an actual editorial process—one that includes accountability for your work.

Your name will go on everything you write. More than that, your name will appear in a publication that is bigger than you are, and you suddenly represent it. You wind up bearing some of the responsibility to make sure that nobody looks like an idiot at the end of the day. Your voice is their voice, and a bit of vice versa. That means being accountable for *everything* you say. Maybe it means not making every mean-spirited joke that comes to mind—sure, it might be funny, but is it fair? Is it something that the publication is going to agree with you on, and if not, can you handle being overruled? Is what you want to say—particularly if it's to the extreme of very good or very bad—worth going to the mat for saying?

This is not to say that you can't or shouldn't vent your spleen or deliver the literary equivalent of a nasty kidney punch when it's warranted. It's just a reminder that you will have to defend that attack—to the editors, to the readers, maybe to the company itself. In short, you're going to have to think before you speak.

A lot of writers fancy themselves to be clever and snarky and, hey, let's face it, smash-mouth copy is fun to read. A vicious beatdown of a bad game can be really entertaining. However, does that really help a gamer decide how to spend their money? Suddenly the goal of looking cool has taken precedence over the goal of getting the job done. If the criticism is no longer constructive, you're going to have trouble with the accountability. Make sure your article will stand up to scrutiny. People are free to disagree with your opinion (and in the age of Twitter, blogs, and YouTube, anybody can give you direct negative feedback at any time), but if they can prove that your facts are wrong or that you haven't supported that opinion, you're toast. And that editor won't be calling you back.

On a human level, the best thing to remember when you're ready to uncork a nasty slam is that you should, can, and will meet the creator of the game that you just trashed with a low score and a lot of pithy insults. There's a human being behind every release. You may not meet them for years, but the game industry is small enough and people change roles often enough that you will stand a good chance of meeting that person at a press event, trade show, or private demo. If you've done a particularly cruel review of one of their other games, they will probably remember you by name. Suddenly, you will find yourself accountable for every nasty thing you said and, unlike the Internet or the safety behind a printed page or a collection of pixels, you will have to handle this confrontation face to face.

I nearly got to live my own advice on this. I gave an outspoken independent designer's game a very, very low score, and he took me to task on several public web forums. He was livid—he made a number of wrong assumptions about how I'd approached my job and called me all manner of extremely nasty names in the process. I didn't respond publicly (but man, was I tempted). Ultimately, he wrote to the publication directly to express his displeasure, and I was able to respond to his concerns privately, with more detail that further explained and supported my original article. I offered to speak to him on a podcast or something, but he declined the offer. We discussed things in email, but I never got to address him live and in person—but I would still welcome that opportunity. I'm not looking for a fight; I'm simply taking the responsibility for my actions and opinions. It's part of the job.

Keep your own developer showdown in mind whenever you do a final proofread of your work. That meeting *will* happen. Just be sure you know what you'll say.

KNOWING THE SCORE
What's the midpoint between 1 and 10?
(Hint: It's not 7)

One of the toughest and certainly most controversial parts of reviewing a game is assigning it a score. Developers and industry critics may not like it, but the majority of the audience wants and expects a quick gauge to compare different titles against each other, and a numerical scale works well—0 or 1 through 10, with various midpoints in between. Sometimes you'll see a certain number of stars, other times you'll see letter grades like you'd find on a school report card. Scores also make things easier for aggregate sites like Metacritic and GameRankings to come up with an average rating across several dozen review outlets. "What did the world think about *Alien Shot*?" "Well, it says here it got a 76 overall." Some people hate Metacritic and everything it stands for, but it's an enormously powerful metric in the games industry and can't be lightly dismissed.

The main problem with review scores is that they are easily abused. Some companies use those score averages to hand out financial bonuses to the development teams; if you get a high enough score, your kid gets braces. But the scoring system wasn't created with dental work in mind. And what's that B+ on one magazine's scale mean in numbers? I was told there would be no math.

And even when two publications use the same system—say, a 10-point scale—many break those numbers down differently, if not completely redefine them. GamesRadar and *Edge* use whole numbers 1 through 10, while GameSpot uses half-points (technically a 20-point scale). *PC Gamer* uses the 100-point scale, leading gamers to debate the empirical superiority of an 8.2 compared to an 8.3. Some outlets find scoring such a tricky business that they change their scales; the American edition of *Official Xbox Magazine* went from a 100-point scale to a 20-point scale (1 through 10 with half-points), but also considered (but never implemented) whole numbers for a time.

Still others make up their own rules. *Game Informer* uses its own 40-point scale: 10 points with quarters (which results in unique scores like 4.75 and 8.25) and calls 7-scoring games "average" instead of the numerical midpoint of 5 or 5.5. That doesn't make much sense to me, but they are consistent about it, which is more important. Meanwhile, 1UP.com chooses to rate everything with report-card style letter grades, leading to B+ and C- reviews. All these systems are valid. It's pretty obvious that this score business is neither easy nor—ironically—all that definitive.

Of course, there are some people who would like to see the score go away entirely and just let the review tell the tale. For those, you'd have to actually *read* the review...and *understand* it, too! But that idea's time has not come, and it will likely never be the primary form of game reviews (which is a shame, as I really like that idea).

The market has spoken; scores are convenient and valuable to the majority of the audience. Like hockey masks and machetes, review scores can certainly be used for evil, but they were created primarily for positive purposes.

So that's the problem you're inheriting. You're going to have to learn one or more of these review systems if you want to get published. At this point, you should focus on making your scores consistent with the text that supports them, as well as making scores consistent within their own scale. Don't write a review with a lot of negative words and then award the game a 9; it's always best to let your words dictate the score. If you arrive at a score that doesn't feel right, then go back, adjust the text, and re-evaluate where the words and the numbers don't seem to agree. And obviously, if you give one game a 6, don't criticize another game for the same flaws a few months later and give it a 4 or an 8. What is it that makes it feel better or worse than the first game? Does better presentation or skillful use of a license warrant a higher score? Maybe the second game simply used too many concepts from the first, so it deserves less praise? If you are following an established publication's system for your own reviews, read the description of what their scores actually mean. It will usually be posted on an About Us page, or at the beginning of the review section, or maybe near the staff bios.

The single most important thing to remember when you're assigning a score sounds a little corny, but it's true: Your scores should also mean something. Who are you writing for, and what are you trying to tell them? What will your score say about the game, and is it illustrated with clear, concrete examples? The truth is that a 7 doesn't do a lot of good. There certainly are mediocre games, and they deserve mediocre scores, like the neither-good-nor-bad 5, or the "hey, you know, it's okay" 7. But a strongly worded 9 can champion a game with lots of detail about why it's so great and really celebrate what that creative team did right, while a 3 can offer real constructive criticism that shows the reader, the developer, and the publisher exactly where things went wrong. That *means* something. A 7 is easy; justifying a 10 or a 2 is hard. And that should be your goal: Not looking for reasons to give out high or low scores, but fully committing to and illuminating the scores you give. Even the 7s.

Breaking the Law of Averages

Since aggregate sites like Metacritic and GameRankings have become such an easy and popular yardstick for success, you will hear criticism of your review if it falls out of the accepted range shown on an aggregate site. The thinking is simple: Majority rules. If several outlets give the game a score between 7 and 7.5, then that's what the community says the game "should" get in all reviews that follow.

This is, of course, a load of horse crap.

If you're writing your review after a game's been released and several day-one reviews have already been tallied, it's very easy to let yourself be led by the court of popular opinion. But being afraid to be seen as "breaking ranks" is a lousy reason to select a score. Your responsibility is as a reviewer, not a repeater.

So strong is the fear of being outside of the Metacritic or GameRankings sweet spot that your media outlet may have a policy about this; they may simply not want their scores to deviate from the norm. If that's the case, you need to have a conversation with your editor openly and respectfully, but I would encourage you to stay strong. I do not believe anyone should re-evaluate a game just so it stays within the average and assume they are "wrong" if their score falls outside of that range. We need qualified opinions, not homogenized ones.

But the opposite is also true: You should you not go out of your way to stand out by intentionally going wildly higher or lower if your gaming heart and analytical mind are not leading you to the middle. And some sites may have that policy, too—they think they will only stand out if they behave wildly, and they want to get a reputation for *something*, even if it's deviant scoring. Don't fall for that either.

Really, it comes down to this: Don't read other reviews until you've written your own. Trust your own instincts and be ready to defend your position regardless of what you may read, see, or hear beyond your own personal, direct experience with the game. Let the game dictate its score, not the reviewers around you.

Things You Should Never Write in a Review

Scores can only be supported with specific language. These worthlessly clichéd phrases don't help the reader gain clear understanding of your position, so avoid this brainless junk in your writing at all costs:

"Fans of the genre will like it." (Alternate: "Fans might enjoy it, but everyone else should steer clear.")

"The X button is used to [do something], while the right trigger is used to [do something else]."

"The graphics are indescribable..." or "The feeling can't be put into words..."

Calling anything "solid" or "workmanlike"

Calling a game released two years ago "classic"

"This one's a definite rental"

Genre clichés that match the game's genre: "*Middle-of-the-Road Racer* takes the checkered flag" or "*Cephalopod Soccer* is a kick in the grass" or "*Alien Shot II* looks locked and loaded to blast off in September."

"I don't like [element of game] myself, but…"

A checklist of paragraphs that touch on graphics, sound, control, and an overall score. (This was the *GamePro* standard in the late '80s and through the late '90s.)

Clichés can serve one good purpose, however: If you twist them and make them into a new, unexpected joke, reference, or commentary. As part of our common cultural experience, clichés are so widely prevalent that everybody knows what you're going to say once you start to say it. So surprise your audience by leading them somewhere else, in context. They'll enjoy the unexpected kick in the grass.

WHAT ABOUT ART?
Where *The Last Gladiator*, *The Last Express*, and *The Last Supper* finally collide

Remember when we tried to define the writer's role as critic or reviewer or journalist in this whole mess in the first section? Well, it's back, this time to point out another paradox.

Reviewing games as consumer objects is pretty straightforward: You paid $60 for this silver disc, you put it in your machine of choice, and you determine whether or not it was worth your money. When a lot of people read movie reviews, that's the kind of advice they're seeking—is this flick worth 10 bucks of my salary and two hours of my life? But if you perceive a difference between "movie reviewer" and "film critic," you may already see the next question coming.

What about art?

Uh oh. A movie reviewer evaluates *I Now Pronounce You Chuck & Larry*, but a film critic judges *Citizen Kane*. (Sometimes they get together and watch *WALL•E*.) And as a game reviewer, you thought you were mouthing off about a silver disc, but now you're judging someone's artistic statement, as well as all the hopes and dreams that go with it. Can you really give an artistic statement 4 out of 10? Is that fair?

It's more than fair; it's actually required. Art and commerce coexist in all other forms of critique. Sure, the folks who look at a painting and decide what it means or what it says and whether it's worth seeing are not buying the work; they're just commenting on it. But you are dealing with a medium that is inherently for sale, and mass-produced at that. There's nothing wrong with evaluating both the inherent monetary value of a game and interpreting the artistic statement it also contains at the same time. What's more, you should.

Some people do make titles that are more artistically motivated than others. Interacting with titles like *Linger in Shadows* or being asked to navigate the pulsating playfields of *Space Giraffe* are artistic statements in and of themselves, and then there's *Braid*, which takes familiar game mechanics, changes them in subtle and brilliant ways, and makes a powerful statement about narrative and player expectations (not to mention life and love) along the way. That doesn't mean you have to like these art games, of course; you can still give those games bad reviews if you didn't have fun or didn't think the artistic statement was fully formed. It's their statement, but it's your money. Those two forces coexist, whether the creators like it or not.

So...what about art? Acknowledge it, celebrate it, but remember your wallet, too. Your readers are most likely consumers, and they usually want that consumer advice first and foremost, but enlightening them with insights about the artistic merit of a game is among your noblest goals.

LEVEL 2 LEARNING IT

■LEVEL 3■

Getting It

It is time to seek your fortune in the outside world. This is where you learn how to approach a media outlet and ask them to pay you for your work. We'll cover what's expected of you, what you should expect of them, what the game companies expect of you both, and yes, how to get free games.

MAGAZINES OR WEBSITES?

You have two primary outlets for your writing.
Choose wisely.

Do you want to write for a fancy videogame magazine, or do you want to write for a slick, always-updated website? The answer, of course, is yes.

Some gamers can't imagine getting their information from anywhere but the web. It's always there, it's constantly updated with the latest news, and it's rapidly become the main form of written communication between human beings, let alone gamers. Others consider a magazine, with its exclusive reveals and deluxe presentation, to be the steakhouse next to online's burger joint: less immediate, a bit fancier, but worth slowing down to savor.

They're both right. Many predicted the end of gaming magazines with the arrival of the Internet; why would anybody want that old hunk of dead tree? But when you no longer define "magazine" as "dead tree," things change dramatically. The advent of tablet computing has opened the door to digital magazines—all the deluxe layout of a print magazine with all the convenience and portability of digital delivery. European and U.S. gaming magazines like *Edge*, *PC Gamer*, *Official Xbox Magazine*, *GamesMaster*, and *PSM* are currently available via Zinio, Apple's Newsstand app for iPad, or both. Plus, who knows what new editorial products will be born in the tablet era? So don't count game magazines out; just change where you look for them.

Arguably, the web is where gamers currently turn for gaming news. Even a digital magazine can't hope to be timely with a news story unless it's exclusive and kept completely under wraps until the issue comes out. Meanwhile, sites like GamesRadar, GameSpot, and IGN post dozens of articles a day as events happen and as news breaks. And when you just want to know the score of a game, there's nothing easier than typing in its title and seeing what GameRankings and Metacritic have already compiled. The Internet can't be beat for custom-tailored information on demand.

Magazines have a luxury of layout freedom that makes multi-page features more viable and game reveals feel like a big deal. *Game Informer*, for instance, rarely if ever puts a game on the cover that is not a world exclusive premiere for that title. Game publishers love this; they get to see their game treated as the most important thing in the world during that whole month, so magazines often wind up breaking big stories and making the games look extra fancy in the process.

You, as a freelance writer, should be ready to kick butt for either magazines or websites. Know the strengths and weaknesses of each format, but don't assume either one is the only one. Both types of publications want responsible, reliable freelancers who can hit deadlines and basically help make the editorial problems go away. Keep an open mind and be ready to be published anywhere.

Extra, Extra

Don't completely forget about the old guard, either. Newspapers—whether they be daily metropolitan, arts weeklies, or collegiate publications—fall somewhere in the middle between magazines and websites. They are more timely than monthly magazines but still behind online; they have the portable convenience and pacing of print but without the deluxe layout, save for a few papers that print in color. They're often forgotten by new writers, but they are a great way to build experience with editing, a body of work, and a reputation as a writer.

INTERNMENT...UM, I MEAN, INTERNSHIPS

Glitz! Glamour! Neither of these will be yours as an intern, but you might score a job

How about this for a job offer: You get to work really hard on grunt-like tasks for no money and very little respect. After four months, someone might learn your name, and when they do, you quit.

If you said "That sounds like paradise," you gotta get an internship!

It's not glamorous, but an internship is actually one of the most prized positions in publishing. The intern is right there, in the thick of it, as the publication is being created. You get to see it all unfold from the front lines. Nothing beats personal experience.

What will that experience be? Humbling, probably. Sorry, but the intern is rarely asked to review that triple-A title or write the cover feature. Sort the mail? Yep. Answer it? Maybe, or at least pick out the letters that the editors should answer later. Send out prizes to contest winners? Often. Editorial interns may be asked to search through the archives for old articles to reprint or build and maintain an index of all past issues. Most publications keep a permanent game library; someone's got to be the librarian and keep it organized, so that often falls to the intern too. The lists of the locations of collectible items in games and occasional cheat codes are not worth printing if they're not accurate, so the intern might be asked to ferret out and confirm those secrets. If the staff is in crunch time (which is usually all the time), interns are sometimes called on to take screenshots for previews or reviews, especially if those articles were written by freelancers who lack their own capture equipment. And while stories of washing the editors' cars and picking up dry cleaning are a bit overstated for humor's sake, don't be offended if you're asked to run to the store to buy some office supplies or a replacement copy of a missing game. Or, yeah, some coffee. Whatever you are asked to do, be ready to do it without complaint. If you can come up with a better way to do it, suggest it before committing to it. Remember that you are there to make the editors' lives and jobs easier. Don't be the sullen maverick who leaves the magazine in worse shape than you found it.

As an intern, you will be asked to do whatever needs doing, but that doesn't mean you have to do *only* that. If you want to write, ask to write—that's why you're there, isn't it? Don't expect to be invited to write automatically; you'll have to show the interest and ask your supervisor for the chance. Some publications have rules about what kind of content interns can and cannot create, but there's actually a good chance that your 50-word preview on *Alien Shot II* will be published, if for no other reason than you're interested, available, and cheap labor. And if what you write doesn't wind up being published, you'll still be getting what you came for: Advice and feedback on your writing from someone who does what you want to do for a living.

Make the most of your presence in the office, too. Go to every meeting you're allowed, whether it's an internal staff meeting, a brainstorming session, or a product demo. They are all chances to learn, if not pitch your story ideas. Nobody's speaking up to write that movie-licensed kiddie game review? Claim it. It's experience, it's exposure, and it's a great way to build goodwill among the editors who will then remember your name and remember you as a motivated person when it comes time for your job search.

That's your silver lining. How much motivation you show during your internship will directly correlate to whether you're seen as just a seat-filler or a potential full-time employee. Many outlets hire their best interns as full-time staffers when they graduate. Interns are not just the gophers of today; they're the editors of tomorrow.

The Intern Loadout

To get an internship at a game publication, you will need a few things:

A college education (in progress)

You won't need a college education simply to be a game reviewer, but you will likely need one to get an internship. Almost all internships require you to be enrolled in an accredited college program and actively attending classes. (Sometimes you can be in high school and score an internship, but those opportunities are exceedingly rare. Ask about them, but don't count on it.) Most internships will give you college credit for your time and effort spent at the publication; some internships will give you a little money as well. But the primary message is clear: Stay in school.

Geographical proximity

This is usually the hardest part, as there are would-be interns in all 50 states and most of the magazines are in one or two. *OXM,* IGN, *PTOM,*

PC Gamer, GamesRadar, GameSpot, 1UP, *@GAMER,* and a few more are all based in the San Francisco Bay area in California. (The biggest print magazine, *Game Informer,* is in Minnesota.) There are a few other magazines in a few other areas, and of course websites can operate from literally anywhere on earth, but no matter the publication, if you want an internship there, you have to *be* there. Usually, internships are split into three phases: Fall (first semester), spring (second semester), and summer (um, vacation). If you wind up going to college near where one of the magazines is located or can spend the summer with a relative in the Bay Area, this is a heck of a lot easier.

Up to 20 hours a week

Think of your internship as a part-time job—a really low-paying (maybe no-paying), kinda boring part-time job where all the fun happens around you but not necessarily with you. Usually the upper end of time you can spend at the job per week is 20 hours; after that, it gets into sticky legal issues about part-time employee benefits and stuff like that. Even if you are needed for more than 20 hours, you may be sent home because, by law, they can't use you more than your allotted time. But more often, an intern works closer to 10 hours a week—two afternoons.

The desire to work

If being a game editor is not just sitting around and playing games all day, you can be sure that an internship isn't either. You will get the chance to play new games before they come out and you might score a few cool t-shirts, but the bulk of your time will be working, and maybe on mind-numbing tasks. As long as you want to get something out of it (and that something is more than just a few cool t-shirts), you'll do fine.

Apply Yourself

Most of the time, publications will advertise when they need interns. Because it's a job, you'll often find the positions listed on the publisher's website (look in the jobs/careers section). Sometimes you'll see postings on "real" job sites like monster.com and, even more often, craigslist.org. Like any other job listing, you'll get all the info about what they're looking for in an intern and what some of your duties will entail. Just treat it like any other job application. Begs, bribes, and blackmail are all appropriate.

Some publications put out a call to local colleges directly, hoping that the academic staff can recommend some currently enrolled candidates. Ask your teachers and guidance counselors if they have any contacts at local publications and see if they'll pitch you or let you pitch yourself with their blessing.

And hey, it never hurts to just call up and ask. If you live nearby, contact your favorite publication and offer yourself as an intern. Just ask them if they need any or if they're going to need some in the next semester. Showing initiative helps. Think about it: If you know you're signing up for slave labor and you still ask for it, why wouldn't you get the job?

FREELANCING: KNOW YOUR ROLE
You make the money, but you don't make the rules

Your first paying gig as a game reviewer will probably be as a freelancer. Why? Nobody's going to hire you for a full-time gig without experience. (The one exception to this is an internship, but that's its own experience—on-the-job training.) Most writers have to prove themselves first, and the best way to do that is as a work-for-hire freelance writer.

Different publications use freelancers for different things, but they all have one thing in common: Freelancers are assigned the stuff that the editors don't have the time or expertise to do themselves. Chances are the editors would like to, even if it's a crappy game, but they simply can't. Their job requires delegation, and editors often delegate to freelancers.

A freelance assignment can be coverage of news events, attending a product demonstration, going to an "editors' day" (which is essentially the first two things combined, only it lasts several hours), reviews and previews, strategy guides, or feature stories. But it boils down to this: They aren't going to do it themselves, so they're asking you to do it for them. It's not flattering to think that your sparkling, beautiful, original, world-changing text might simply being used as filler, but that's sometimes the truth.

I've been both a freelancer for hire and a hirer of freelancers, and I've come up with some basic truths that may be of use before you dive into the talent pool:

If you want work, you have to ask for it

The first part of getting a job is looking for one. Every so often I see someone on say, "I'm totally available for freelance assignments, call me," on Twitter or a blog, and I roll my eyes. That's absolutely not the way to do it. Editors are busy, remember? They're not scouring the planet, seeking fresh talent. You may be a good writer, but chances are rare that an editor will happen upon your Facebook post where you bemoan the fact that nobody will give you a shot and therefore be inspired to give you one. Also, saying, "Why won't anyone hire me?" is very different from, "Hi, will you hire me?" One shows motivation, and the other does not. We'll get into how to approach an editorial outlet for freelance assignments shortly, but know that good things do not come to those who wait; good things come to those who seek them out.

Don't be a jerk when you ask

Wheaton's Law applies here. Editors want to work with someone who is pleasant and professional. They do not want to hire a person who is here to show them what they are doing wrong. Don't be too cool. Don't be arrogant. Just be polite when you offer to help in exchange for money.

You will get the crap games

Full-time positions at game publications are hard to come by and hard to keep; there's a lot of stress and responsibility. The one comfort that full-timer staffers have is, "At least I get to review *Alien Shot II* when it finally comes out." That means, even though you are a raging *Alien Shot* fanboy, you have played the original *Alien Shot* all the way through four or five times, and you might even be more qualified to review the sequel than the full-timer, you're not going to get the chance. Instead, while the editor handles *Alien Shot II* him or herself, you get *Middle-of-the-Road Racer*.

One reliable freelancer almost talked himself out of a job by telling my publication, "I'm available for the following triple-A, high-profile titles, but I'm really not interested in reviewing other stuff." As a result, he didn't get work from the reviews editor for a long time after that. Choosing his assignments simply wasn't his call to make, and the editor knew there are other writers who wouldn't be so picky. So he hired them instead.

You may not get much warning

Freelancers often have to stay light on their feet, ready for short deadlines. A good assignment with a lot of planning should give you at least a week to complete your task. That said, don't be surprised if you get a call Tuesday asking you for copy by Friday. If you are overextended and cannot complete an assignment, do not accept it. Thank them and just tell them you are booked—it's the responsible thing to do. Chances are good that you will get called upon again if you simply keep it real and keep in touch.

You need to communicate and then not communicate

Once you've got an assignment, ask all your questions up front, and then get out of the editor's hair. Of course, it's always better to ask than to make a mistake that can't be fixed, but if the editor's time is precious, writing daily "what about this?" and "how should I handle this?" emails is not going to endear you to anybody. Find out what you need to know to do your job, and then do it without further assistance, like the independent contractor you are.

There is one huge exception. Sometimes you may need to contact the game publisher to get more information. Here, you should not contact the publisher directly—talk to your editor and tell them what you need. Some editors prefer to be your contact point to the company; others may say, "Give the PR person a call." Be ready for either, but absolutely find out which course of action the editor prefers before you do anything on your own.

You need to follow directions

Sounds obvious, but it's a common mistake. If, in the course of finding out what you need to know to complete the assignment, you receive specific instructions or a template to follow, follow them exactly. Nearly all major outlets have a template for core information—publisher, developer, number of players, score—and while that template may be slightly different at each publication, that template will be consistent within each publication. If the template states that a release date should appear as "January 2084," don't write down "01/15/84." Someone somewhere had a meeting once to determine how the date should appear in the magazine, and it was chosen for a reason—they're not asking you to overrule their decision. All the little things like that count, and minding those details shows that you can be trusted to follow directions. Be creative in your copy, not in your interpretation of the rules.

If you do not receive a template for your review, check out some recent articles from that outlet and mimic the structure that you see on the pages. Publications often get letters from people who say they're really interested in writing, but when a sample is received, absolutely no thought is given to what the publication actually looks like. If you want to impress *Official Game Critics*, don't submit your work following the style of *Game Piñata*. Show that you want to write for *Official Game Critics* by respecting and following *Official Game Critics'* format.

You will need to do research

"Can you handle a review for *Cephalopod Soccer* by next Friday?" If you say yes but have never played a soccer game *or* seen an octopus before, you have your work cut out for you. The only valid opinion is an informed one. Expect that you will have to dust off some older games in your collection or take a trip to your local rental outlet to brush up on other entries in the genre. In the case of sequels/ franchises (particularly relevant in sports), find out what has set the standard and what other choices consumers have faced in the past and will face by the time your review comes out. The magazine or website will not send you a stack of back issues or a handy list of links to all previous relevant reviews; they will expect either that you can find them on your own or that you already have the experience needed to fulfill the obligation you just accepted. For sequels, it's particularly valuable to know what the publication said about the franchise in previous years. If your sequel review calls the first game "disappointing" but the outlet you're writing for gave it a high score, you'll look stupid and maybe even offend your new employer.

You need to hit deadlines

Assume there is no padding in the date you have been given. Assume that the editor is giving you up until the utter last moment to hand in your sparkling, beautiful, original, world-changing article so that it can be all the more sparkling, beautiful, original, and world-changing. Ask for an extension only under exceptional circumstances. These circumstances include the death of a loved one or your very own death. The freelancers who get taken seriously are the freelancers who take deadlines seriously. (Seriously.)

Furthermore, competing deadlines are never an excuse. *GameBloviator* does not care at all about your commitments to *Bloviate Gamer*. Assume they are bitter rivals engaged in a blood feud, and bringing one up to the other will only make it look like you do not consider your current employer a priority.

If you really want to make an impression, beat the deadline. Turn in your sparkling, beautiful, original, world-changing article a day early. Your editor may fall madly in love with you.

Your copy needs to be super-clean

The reason you were hired is because the editor didn't have the time to do it themselves, but they certainly have the ability. If you turn in an article that they have to severely rewrite, they will not call you back. They will have realized, "Hey, for the amount of time it took me to rewrite this, I could have written it from scratch myself!" That's not always true, but it's what they'll think and maybe even say out loud. Either way, you're screwed. Every step as a freelancer has to be with your best foot forward.

What's more, when you submit your article, make sure everything is organized. Don't submit screenshots with obscure or generic names; call your files AlienShot_01.jpg through AlienShot_05.jpg, then match the captions in your review to those specific file names. Make it easy for the people who will work with your files to match them up in the final layout. Double-check that you're using the right template and that you have followed its structure. Little things mean a lot, and anything like this that the editor has to fix or change will be remembered in a negative light.

You probably won't make a ton of money

Each publication sets its own pay rates; there is no universal standard, but 50 cents a word is generally considered pretty good pay. Less than 50 cents a word is very common. A buck a word is heaven, and you may only see that from mainstream publications (that is, national publications not aimed directly at videogame enthusiasts) who are dealing with a mass market and a different economy of scale.

Some outlets simply set a price of X amount per page or article, then adjust it based on the specific assignment. You may get X for a full-page review, but you may get slightly less if you don't take your own screenshots (more on this later), and you may get fractions of the full-page rate for fractional reviews that only take up 1/2 or 1/3 of the magazine page. Keep in mind that you always want to be busy as a freelancer, and multiple assignments at less-than-optimal rates will actually do a better job of paying the bills. Pump up the volume.

If there's one statement that summarizes the role of a freelancer, it's this: *You exist to make the editor's job easier.* It's not necessarily fair, easy, glamorous, or particularly fun. But as a freelancer, you have to accept it. It's the nature of the job.

And Then Everything Broke

There is one notable complication you might run into when you've been assigned a review for a product that is still several weeks away from release: game-breaking bugs. When you see problems like missing textures, insanely long load times, or wacky physics in a game, you have the added challenge of trying to figure out whether the not-quite-100%-final game is acting up because of a problem that's already been fixed by the developers, or if it's going to act up on every gamer who buys it because of a programming mistake.

This is not a decision you have to make on your own. Contact your editor and explain what you've found; if it sounds serious enough, they will contact the company and ask about it on your behalf. It's a little dicey because now you're tipping your hand; you normally would not tell a publisher "here's a problem I've found with your game" before they read the review. But if the disc you put in the drive says "95% build" or came with a list of caveats and known issues that are going to be addressed by the time your review appears—or if they simply say, "Yes, we spotted that right after we sent you the disc, and it's already been fixed"—then you ethically have to give them the benefit of the doubt. By all means, if you feel like it's too big of an issue to fairly ignore, ask your editor if it's possible to delay the review until you can get an updated build. The answer may ultimately be "no," but your editor will at least respect your integrity.

Mind you, I've brought up some serious issues during my reviews and been told by the publishing company, "Oh yeah, that's going to be fixed," and many times it wasn't fixed when I played the retail version, but that's a risk you have to take. You must trust that you are being told the truth. If you slam a game for a mistake that isn't there in the final product, it's worse than if you neglect mentioning a problem that you honestly believed was going to be addressed. And because you brought it up ahead of time, your editor will be able to have your back if someone presses them on why this obvious bug wasn't mentioned in the review, and it can be addressed officially in the letter column or as an editor's note on the review later. You will have done the responsible thing.

If you're reviewing a retail disc and the game crashes or you see big obvious bugs, then by all means, go to town. Lots of people gave that game the green light before it reached your hands, and now your responsibility is solely to the audience.

"BUT I'M ALREADY PERFECT!"

You're going to be edited.
Better get used to it.

We talked about self-editing before, and it is a crucial skill. But no matter how perfect your writing is, someone else will make it more perfect. And it will happen on every article you write.

Some editors do not feel like they are doing their job unless they have changed your copy. This is not your problem to solve, but it is your reality to accept, if not expect. I worked with one of those editors early in my career, and it drove me nuts because sometimes he would change a tiny little bit—a turn of phrase, a synonym, something small that would neither improve nor destroy the article either way, but it was no longer entirely mine. And I think the editor simply felt, "Well, by changing this part of the article, I can prove that I did what I was hired to do—I actively edited this article." Maybe it was OCD, maybe it was CYA—whatever the reason, that was just the way he worked. I quickly stopped getting offended about my wonderful words being arbitrarily changed. I was still proud of the resulting articles.

Other times, of course, I was edited because my work needed editing. Sometimes when you do your best, your best is not really good enough. It's extremely important to go into a freelance assignment knowing that you are there to serve that magazine's needs and that your voice is part of their larger chorus. It is their responsibility, even more than their right, to change your words—or even your scores—for the better of the outlet they represent. Editors who respect you will contact you with major changes of phrasing or rating so you have a heads-up, but you simply can't be offended that they are doing their jobs.

Ultimately, it's another facet of knowing your role and accepting that you cannot control your work once you place it in someone else's hands. Trust will be built between you and your editor as you learn each other's styles and expectations, and you may soon find that your articles are subject to lighter and lighter edits as you progress—but those first few should be seen as learning experiences. Don't focus on what they changed, but why they changed it. Compare your version with theirs and reverse-engineer the edits; they were not arbitrary. Did they add detail that makes your statements more clear? Did they remove superfluous detail that cluttered things up? Maybe it wasn't about your writing at all; maybe the article was altered for reasons of space, not content.

If you have serious questions about why something was changed, you can always ask the editor. Just let them know that you noticed how it changed and you'd like to hit the target closer next time, so if they can spare a few moments to explain, you want to give them less to edit on the next assignment. Phrasing it that way will almost certainly get you a useful response. Being defensive about the edit or phrasing it as "how dare you change my words" is going to be met with…less enthusiasm. Publications will not work with a freelancer who is precious about their copy. They just don't need the hassle of your ego second-guessing their expertise.

Now…what if they change your article for the worse? Maybe your editor changes something you've said so it doesn't sound authentic, or perhaps they've even altered your meaning, or worse, your judgment of the game itself. In these cases, the editor should be contacting you with any questions about ambiguity in your copy or a simple difference of opinion.

However, while giving you a call or dashing off a quick email is the responsible and professional course of action, you cannot guarantee that they will actually reach out to you. In those cases, you need to contact them and discuss it directly—and privately. There have been a few high-profile instances of freelancers who decided that the best way to deal with the discrepancies between what they wrote and what was printed was to go on a blogging spree and post their original version while accusing the publication of unethical behavior. The results have not been pretty. Not only does every wannabe writer on the Internet grab popcorn for a good e-fight and get to act superior, but the writer often gets quietly but unofficially blacklisted.

Remember, you are an employee for hire; you are getting work because the editorial outlet wants your voice in the mix. If your voice suddenly says, "These guys are jerks," obviously you're going to alienate the publication in question—the one you never want to write for again—but you are also sending out a signal to everybody else who might have considered hiring you. You are damaged goods in a writing pool with endless options; if you attacked *Official Game Critics* in public, why should the staff at *Game Piñata* expect to be treated any differently? The games media talks amongst itself and it looks out for its own. Your freelance career is hereby over.

Here's a very real example: Some years back there was a very public disagreement between a freelance reviewer and a large, popular website for which he'd written. The writer's scores were changed from a very low score to a middling score, because the editor felt the game deserved a bump up. Scores were changed and some extra phrases were added (presumably for balance), the writer posted angrily about it on a blog, and the Internet was treated to allegations concerning the site's allegiance to advertisers, the nature of the role of an editor, and other weighty issues. But all the editor had to do was call the writer before the changes were posted, and failing that, the writer should have had the decency to call the editor and voice his disapproval privately instead of going public. Even the site admitted that it was an unfortunate breakdown in communication between the editor and the writer. Ultimately the review was taken down and the angry blog post was removed. So... all that for nothing, and one gesture by either side probably could have resolved it with less muss and fuss. It's a worthwhile lesson.

For your own sake, if you feel you've been mistreated with a botched edit, don't go rogue, no matter how offended you are. Take it up directly with your editor, like a professional should, and discuss it.

These kinds of situations are rare, though; more often, you'll find your articles are slightly tweaked, reasonably reworded, amended for detail, or simply edited for space. In the end, learning from your edits is in your best interest. Swallow that pride and keep working—and you'll keep working.

KNOW YOUR MASTHEAD
Talk to the right person at a publication or you're talking to the wall

Sure, you want to be a staff member at a media outlet—but which person do you want to be? Before you go writing (or worse, calling) the staff at your favorite publication inquiring about a job, you need to know who does what and which person to contact.

Start with the *masthead*. For websites, check for a link called Staff or About Us. For magazines, check the first few or last few pages, and you'll find a listing of the staff along with legal bits about how many times a year the magazine is published and/or who owns the publication. Sometimes the masthead contains information on how to reach the customer service department (handy when the mailman steals your issue or when you can't access the subscription section of a website) and how to reach the advertising sales staff (handy when you have a videogame to sell and would like to move several million copies of it by the holidays). But as a freelancer, you only want to focus on the editorial staff listing. One day, with luck, you'll find yourself working your way up its ranks.

There is one big caveat, though: Every outlet is different. Some websites have all the positions listed below; others might only have four or five. The duties listed are typical but not absolute, and some titles mean different things in different publications. On the small staff of *Flux*, I was dubbed the Managing Editor but my duties were more like a Senior Editor or an Executive Editor. So don't be surprised if you make contact with one person and get shuffled off to another in short order; each editorial outlet has its own balance of power and chain of command. As long as you ask smart, polite questions, you can find out what it is fairly easily.

Editor-in-Chief
AKA: The Boss

As you probably already know, the EiC calls the shots. It's their job to give the writing a consistent voice, to land the big stories, to steer the ship. They're expected to not only lead the team of editors and provide feedback, advice, and one-to-one editing sessions with their crew, but they also write reviews, features, previews, and strategies, and they brainstorm on all of the above. Plus they are the main conduit between the editorial staff and the other departments, such as advertising, circulation, and production. They are also the one who takes the blame when things go wrong—fact-checking errors, companies who feel their products were not given proper consideration or were not reviewed fairly, angry letters from outraged readers and parents. It's a lot of work and pretty stressful. Some EiCs choose their magazine's cover stories; others are simply asked to create a story around a hot title or concept by a committee. It all depends on the outlet.

If a magazine lacks an EiC, their duties often get sprinkled around to everyone else, especially the executive editor. Sometimes you might find someone simply called the "editor" with no prefix or suffix; if it's above the executive editor on the masthead, they're probably acting as EiC for the time being. Often it's as simple as that person not having enough applicable experience to be granted the "in chief" title, or maybe they've been put in charge of a special issue but will go back to their regular duties once that project is completed.

The EiC is usually the only editorial position that has a chance to deliver a six-figure paycheck. Don't count on it, and know that it won't come without several years of experience. Anybody who thinks that videogame writing is the fast track to fame and fortune, know that you'll probably have to settle for fame. And, um, not much of that.

Executive Editor

AKA: The Right Hand (Wo)Man

The EE is Chewie to the EiC's Han Solo—or if you're on the other side of the geek fence, Riker to Picard. (If you don't like either *Star Trek* or *Star Wars*, find another job.) They are responsible for helping with all of the above. It's not that the EiC is unapproachable; it just helps to have a wingman. Because the EiC is often called on to travel, speak to the media, or attend upper-level management meetings, you want someone around who can answer questions, tweak copy, generate stories based on what the day calls for, and generally run the ship while the commander is away. They're also expected to help keep things on schedule, help interface with the other departments, and generally know what the hell is going on. Executive editors probably directly manage the senior editors, sometimes coordinate the freelance writer pool, and may be responsible for an intern or two.

Some publications don't have an Executive Editor; *GamePro*, for instance, operated without one for about a decade. In cases like that, the EE duties trickle down to the other editors below.

Senior Editor

AKA: The Mentor

Senior editor is where perks and responsibility come together. They're high enough on the food chain to enjoy the cool stuff, like free t-shirts and the occasional fun business trip, yet they have enough influence at the magazine to make their voice heard in every issue. Senior editors are expected to lead by example, and they're also called upon to work with freelancers and younger staff writers to help improve their copy. It's practically a teaching position.

Senior editors could be asked to do anything—writing features, visiting developers and publishers, hosting game demos, running staff meetings, managing interns, brainstorming ideas, contacting companies for updated information and builds of software, producing a podcast, planning and editing sections of the magazine or website, researching facts, you name it. Senior editors rarely have final say on anything (let's not forget everybody listed up until this point) but if they have a good idea, they can throw it out there in a meeting with a supporting argument, and it can often gain traction. The EiC and EEs look to them to be...I don't want to say camp counselors, but that's sort of what it is. Maybe sergeants? Senior editors often manage the "younger" editors on staff, or might run the intern pool, so it's where the work changes from purely creative output to a blend of writing and people skills. And not only do they get to nurture new talent, but they get to show off and review the high-profile games!

Senior editors can influence a lot of areas of the publication and are called on to help with most of them at one time or another. Of all the positions I've held, this was actually the most fun, because I really felt like I was knee-deep in *making* something.

Associate Editor

AKA: The Workhorse

If there are senior editors, who are the junior editors? You guessed it. Associates are responsible for a lot of the grunt work—previewing games, writing up news stories, tracking down details like the number of levels in a game, calling companies for new screenshots, stuff like that. The duties are pretty similar to the assistant editor, but the associate generally has a little bit more responsibility, like planning/writing a section of the publication or acting as a liaison to a slightly higher-profile game publisher. That said, nothing's off limits—previews, reviews, strategies, feature stories, news, answering mail, you name it. If it needs doing, the associate editor is expected to do it, even if they have to learn it as they go with some guidance from a higher-level staffer.

The upside is that associates get a lot of interesting experiences to go with their expected versatility. They might attend game demos or "editor days" where publishers show the press a whole bunch of games in one sitting and offer some fun social activities as a by-product. Some outfits have a senior associate editor, too, especially if there are a lot of associates on staff.

Assistant Editor

AKA: N00b

If you've just been hired, this is likely your title, and at least it's more official-sounding than "Intern Plus." Assistants still get plenty of grunt work, like taking screenshots and attending the demos and events that nobody else wants to deal with. Assistant editors can and will write a lot, so it's the prime time to polish their writing skills. They'll probably report to a senior editor, and that's part of the reason why: They're likely to benefit from a writing coach. They get to see all the latest games first, sit in on any game demo they like, start making friends and contacts in the industry, and they get paid. They also pay their dues, but you don't hear assistant editors complain too much because they know they're building a career.

Those are the juicy positions—the content editors most people are thinking about when they talk about how cool it would be to work at a videogame magazine or website. There are other positions on the masthead you should know about, maybe because you might be good in those roles, but also so you know what *not* to do when you see them.

Managing Editor

AKA: The Traffic Cop

Whereas most editorial positions focus on generating content, the managing editor is more about procedure. It's their responsibility to keep the publication on its production schedule, even more so than the executive editor (and they're usually on par or slightly below the EE in terms of staff hierarchy). The managing editor watches the calendar and works to make sure the articles have been edited, fact-checked, and fully designed. In print, they make sure pages are ultimately delivered to the production department, ready for shipping to the printer; they'll also get those pages back when production has done its final tweaks and adjustments, and they'll need to sign off on each page of the magazine before it's sent out. Online, managing editors ensure that the articles are posted to the site on the agreed schedule (and not, catastrophically, before an embargo lifts) and the content flows steadily. In either case, they are generally the last line of defense against mistakes. They're usually in charge of one or more copy editors as well (or they might be the default copy editor), and they might be the contact point for freelancers if that doesn't fall within the executive editor's duties.

Managing editors are also the arbiters of the style guide, a collection of writing rules and regulations that nearly every publication follows. Style guides vary by publication, but it's the managing editor's job to maintain the one for their specific domain.

Because the managing editor is so often aware of the deadlines, it's one of the more stressful jobs, and it rarely comes with the attention that content editors receive. (Not that managing editors can't write articles, too; many do, in addition to their regular duties; they *have* to be good writers at their core to do their job.) However, the role of managing editor is perfect for people who really value being part of and helping to lead a team and want to put their organizational skills to the test. To the right candidate, it's extremely rewarding and an absolutely vital role on the staff.

Copy Editor
AKA: Grammar Rodeo Buckaroo

Think of a managing editor, then strip away the obsession with scheduling and replace it with an obsession over punctuation and dangling participles, and you've got a copy editor. The copy editor has to know and love the nuts and bolts of the language; if you don't dot your i's and cross your t's, they will do it for you and then ask you (politely) to get it right the next time. If the managing editor is the last line of defense against typos, the copy editor is the first, so attention to detail is an absolute must. And while this, too, is a position that doesn't get much glory, copy editors can and often will write articles. I know two copy editors who switched gears slightly to become full-time content editors—and everybody wanted to "edit" their work, because quite often, no editing was necessary.

Reviews Editor, Features Editor, News Editor, Tech Editor/Hardware Editor, Online Editor, Channel Editor, Platform Editor

AKA: Section Editor

This one's self-explanatory—they do what their title says they do. They're in charge of reviews or previews or, in the case of a platform editor, anything to do with a specific console or device. Sometimes this crosses over with senior editor titles, so you might see a publication with a "senior editor, technology" and "senior editor, reviews" or you might just see the section as the job title. But they're in charge of that section of the website or magazine, whether they write it themselves or use freelancers to generate the content and then edit it for publication. On a print magazine, online editor generally means they're the person who bridges the print and website content, or writes stuff about one realm for the other.

Contributing Editor/Contributing Writer

AKA: Freelancer

"Contributing"—that's the code word for "person who doesn't work here but whose name appears on articles." Whether they are called an editor or a writer is entirely up to the staff and how much respect they want to bestow on that person, or how often they contribute. If a freelancer is contracted to do a certain number of articles per month, then they might score the editor title more easily than someone who writes intermittently. Then again, some publications just like to have one name for everybody who freelances for them, regardless of what they actually did.

Editor-at-Large

AKA: The Free Spirit

The editor-at-large writes what they want to write. Usually it's a high-profile freelancer or ex-EiC who has a long-term relationship with the publication and generates significant content on a regular basis, but they don't handle any of the day-to-day stuff of running the magazine or website. The editor-at-large title usually comes with some sort of special creative freedom, such as a regular column about whatever tickles their fancy, the opportunity to travel and represent the publication at industry conferences or events, the ability to be selective about what they want to write, stuff like that. Due to the creative freedom, it's a title that's earned, not applied for.

Editorial Director

AKA: Overlord

Editorial director is more of an overseeing role. This person probably isn't involved in the day-to-day writing of the content, but is there as an advisor, a go-between for the business side (publisher) and the editorial side (editor-in-chief). They help with big-picture stuff, like how a magazine cover is constructed and where the website's editorial voice fits in the marketplace. Editorial directors are usually people who have served as editors (and often editors-in-chief) for several years and are now being asked to oversee multiple projects. Generally, they're not a person who can help you get hired. They're a bit too busy. Leave them alone.

Publisher

AKA: The Money

There's an old adage that if you want results, you have to go to the top. But when it comes to media outlets, for crying out loud, don't. The publisher is not the person to write to ask for a job or an internship, unless he's a friend of your family, and in that case, you probably don't have to write them. The publisher deals with the macro elements of running the business—fun stuff like budgets, market trends, ad sales, readership, the competition, and staff fluctuations. The publisher often hires and fires people, but they're not going to hire *you*. Leave them to the business of business; if you write them begging for a job, your letter will, at best, be shuffled off to the editor-in-chief or the general mailbag. At worst, it's thrown away. Assume the worst.

So who *should* you write to ask for a job? Your best and most appropriate bets are the executive editor or managing editor. They are often the people charged with hiring freelancers. It might be a senior editor, especially if the masthead does not show an executive editor.

The other good way to find out who to write is to simply call the publication. Dial the main number, and you'll often get the receptionist. Sometimes they know who handles new freelancer requests, or they'll call a staff member to find out. And if you need the number, figure out who's publishing the magazine or website and find it from there. Use some info-gathering skills, for cryin' out loud—if you can't find the phone number for the place you want to work, you're not going to have the skills to get the info for the stories you'll need to write, either.

If you want to get your foot in the door as a new writer, it's not what you know, and it's not even who you know; it's what you know about who does what.

HELLO, PLEASE PAY ME TO PLAY GAMES
Get ready to throw your first pitch

Gaming editors get lots of reader feedback through many sources, and a good amount of it is from young writers looking for their first big break. Trouble is, that's not something the editors particularly want to get. It's not easy to get noticed, and the editors are definitely not going to call you first.

When an editor needs a new writer—freelancer or staff candidate—they generally go with the people they already know and trust. If a writer doesn't immediately leap to mind, they then ask their staff or their trusted friends for recommendations. And failing that, a classified ad is placed (often on the local Craigslist, so as to attract someone who already lives nearby and won't have to be relocated at great expense) and, usually in the case of a permanent position, the job availability is listed on the company website.

This makes the guy who lives 2000 miles away sending out-of-the-blue emails asking for money something of a longshot.

So, strategy is pretty important at this stage. When you feel you've got the practice, you've got the talent, and you've got the good old-fashioned gumption—not to mention the address of the editorial publication you want to approach—follow these eight hundred simple steps.

Make yourself easy to contact

Before you even start sending out feelers, establish your lines of professional communication. Your online gamer nickname might be D3v4ztat0r, and you may be proud that it's also your email address—but you can't cash a check made out to D3v4ztat0r. It's worth getting an email account in your real name before making your first business contact, assuming you don't want to register and use your name as a domain (which many full-time freelancers choose to do). You want the editors to know who you really are and remember your real name, so reinforce it with a smart choice from the beginning. If you have a cell phone, use that as your business line and change the outgoing message to reflect your new role—"If you're calling regarding an assignment or a pitch, please leave your number, or you can send an email to JohnDoeWriter at gmail dot com."

Be specific and play to your strengths

Don't say you like all kinds of games. You don't—as with music, there's at least one genre that makes your stomach turn, one that you take great pains to avoid, one that's not represented in your personal collection at all. You have a favorite genre, and you know you have a favorite genre. Tell them what it is. RPGs often take so much time and effort to play through that they are first to be freelanced out; the editor has other things to do, but a freelancer is being paid to sit at home and march through 150 hours of gameplay. If this is a particular strength of yours, say so. Similarly, sports, fighting, and wrestling games often require an intimate knowledge of the history of the franchises that a staff editor may or may not have; they can fake it, but they'd rather get an expert to speak for the publication and not look foolish. And you never know—maybe the publication doesn't currently have anybody on staff who knows bass fishing games really well, and they could use a freelancer to fill that niche. If you have a specialty or an area of expertise, it's in your best interest to let them know.

Do not offer to work for free at a publication that pays

This is the sign of a total amateur. You may be thinking, "But I am so eager, I will do whatever it takes to prove myself!" But the editor is thinking, "This person clearly doesn't know how we do things in the big leagues...and if it's so bad he has to give it away, I sure as hell don't want it." The trick, then, is not to mention money at all. This is your first introduction. Money comes after you've been hired—and after you've done the job right.

Show your best stuff

You know that old saying and popular deodorant commercial: You never get a second chance to make a first impression. If you're going to send a writing sample, send your best work. Focus your submissions on games released within the last year, but don't send your most recent work just because it's fresh; they don't care what the last game was that you rented. They care that the game you analyzed was done so with skill and an attention to detail.

Target your unpublished writing samples

Even if you've got one stock review of *Alien Shot* that you really like and want to use as your calling card, tailor it to each publication you pitch. That is, if the mag or site you want to write for uses a rating scale of 1 to 10 by whole numbers, don't send them an unpublished sample review with a score of 8.7 on it. If the website doesn't give an arbitrary rating to Replay Value, don't include it in your sample. Make your samples match their template as best you can just by reading their existing pages. This shows a familiarity with the product that you are saying you want to help create—you're contacting them because you want to write for that specific publication—and it avoids the sense that you are just some desperate newbie eager to please anybody who will respond to your beg for work. (Of course, you and I know that that's exactly what you are at this point—any port in a storm, right? You just don't have to make it so obvious.)

Published is published

It might be the school newspaper, it might be a free arts weekly, it might be a local daily paper, but they all count as professional writing forays. The appropriate term is "regionally published," and they're all valid as examples of what you can do. A writing sample that obviously comes from a publication, even a small one, shows two things: You are already good enough to get published, and you have already worked with an editor. A photocopy of your work as it appeared in a newspaper is more powerful than a plain Microsoft Word document.

The flip side of this is fanzines. Unless they look exceptionally professional, don't bother. If you like what you've written, better to submit it as if it were an unpublished sample and mention that you've done some work for fanzines, or note where this sample originally appeared at the bottom of the review.

Presentation isn't the most important thing, but it helps

If you're submitting writing samples via email, supply direct links
to your published work—not the home page of the site, but a link
straight to your article. If you don't have published work, create
a simple HTML version and post it on your website; if you send
attachments, send them as platform-agnostic RTF or PDF files. While
most outlets use Microsoft Word, do not assume that the publication
uses the same word-processing software you do. Differences
between operating systems and software versions can make your
document unreadable, and no editor will struggle to crack open a
mystery file from an unknown hopeful.

If you're submitting printed samples via mail or fax, don't. In
this day and age, they'll simply be ignored. It's not hard to create
PDFs of your published work, so do the minor research required and
learn how to make them, then upload them as attachments or make
them available as downloadable links from your website.

If you are submitting unpublished work, at least make it look
pretty in your word processing program. If you (or a friend) have
layout skills and a little time, you can whip something up in a
design program like QuarkXpress or InDesign and generate a PDF
for submission. HTML will work in a pinch too. Honestly, it doesn't
have to be fancy, it just has to be organized and easy to read.

Don't bury the editors

Two or three examples of your best work should suffice; any more
will be ignored and will dilute your strength. I've been sent seven
and eight links to different articles around the web, but I don't have
time to go through all that, and the list looks intimidating enough
for me to want to skip it altogether. I also take it as a sign of bloated
indecision on the writer's part (not a good sign in a career where
being able to cut things even when you don't want to cut them

is a key skill). Depending on the context, it can even come off as arrogant—"I'm good enough for you to want to read everything I've ever written! You simply must stop what you're doing and read *all* of my golden prose!"

The editor is a busy person, so they might spend five minutes reading your samples, 10 if you're lucky. They just want a feel for how your voice would mesh with their existing message—how *you* will fit with *them*, not the other way around. It's best to give them freedom *from* choice and use the magic phrase "More samples are available upon request." And honestly? If they like your two or three samples, the fourth one they read may be your first assignment for them.

Don't sweat the résumé

You should include one, because your potential employer wants to know what your life experience is and whether or not it applies to your writing career, but your writing samples will actually be the most valuable thing you send. After submitting a pitch packet to a magazine that later hired me, I found out that they only really used the résumé for the contact information—phone number, email, etc. The rest of the page went unnoticed. However, if they can scan the page and see phrases like "journalism major," "campus newspaper," or "regionally published," those are all worth putting down.

Stay professional

Send them a résumé, some samples, and a letter of introduction. That's all you need; anything else is probably overkill and can work against you. Knowing the staff's professed love for a certain high-caffeine soft drink, I once sent a résumé rolled up in an empty Mountain Dew bottle. I figured that would get me noticed—"hey, look, I read your magazine, and I care about the little details you mention. I'll show you I'm a fan and stroke your ego at the same time." Well, schtick like that may be creative, but it didn't work for me and, now that I've spent some time on the other side, I can tell you that it probably won't work for you, either. It's the sign of someone who values flash over content, and it goes right into the garbage...after, of course, the recipient shouts to the rest of the staff, "Hey, check it out, some idiot sent a résumé in a Mountain Dew bottle—how desperate is *that*?" *Then* they throw it away. Better to let your work make your mark.

Show personality

You don't have to go as far as stupid stunts with your résumé, but you should not write a cover letter or introductory email so dry that you look lifeless and uninteresting as a writer. Let them know you are a real live person. On the flip side, don't go too far for a joke ("It's-a me, your new-a freelancer!" isn't going to get you hired, *ever*) and don't try to shoehorn in tons of insider gaming references to show them that you're hardcore. Your hardcoreness is assumed. Careful use of a conversational tone can help you more, and a little subtle humor can make you memorable. And always remember to keep it brief—your potential editor doesn't have time to wade through three paragraphs of your life story, or how much you love *Halo*, or why you're great. Be sharp, be focused, be confident, and you'll make the best impression possible.

Don't brag about your gaming prowess

It's assumed that you know the up end of a joystick. Being at the top of an Xbox Live leaderboard won't help you one bit when it comes to actually putting words together. Editors know this. By this point in the book, you should too.

Ask for a style guide and writer's guidelines

Every magazine and website does things just differently enough to cause freelancers infinite trouble. But generally, the managing editor keeps the guidelines that all writers, staff and freelance alike, should follow. This includes things like spelling of specific terms, deadline expectations, payment terms, and other important stuff. Asking for writer's guidelines and a copy of the style guide shows you at least know there will be rules to follow and that you are prepared to follow them.

For heaven's sake, spell things right

The first thing you can do to lose this job is to send a letter, résumé, or writing sample with mistakes in it. If you're not willing to polish your pitch letter—on which all your hopes for success are currently riding—why would an editor assume you would be any more diligent on the articles you'd submit to them? You are approaching this publication saying "I have a wicked command over the English language." Not knowing how to spell those fancy SAT words says exactly the opposite, plus it suggests you are sloppy and do not pay attention to details. I have seen entire résumés and pitch packets tossed into the recycle bin because of a single typo. If you want to write prose for the pros, do it right from the start. And if u want ne1 2 notice u, don't write in text message lingo, leetspeak, or any other online chat slang, because u will n3var g3t h1r3d.

Bring your own ideas

Most of your freelance work will probably be reviews, but editors are tasked with constantly creating a stream of new stories for their publications. It can be exhausting, and sometimes, a fresh idea from a freelancer with the time to develop it is exactly what an editor wants to hear. Remember: From the editor's point of view, freelancers exist to help solve problems. The best thing an editor can hear is a turnkey solution to a problem they face every day. Don't push too hard on first contact, but if you have an interesting approach to a review or a short feature idea that you think would be a good match, it's okay to ask if they'd be interested in it.

Don't send one email to the whole staff

It's an understandable mistake, but it's the sign of a frantic rookie. They will all assume someone else is taking care of it and ignore it, including the person who should have gotten it in the first place. Figure out which person should really read it (using the tips in the previous chapter) and send it just to them.

Politely follow up after you send in your stuff

Email is good, assuming you can survive the spam filter. You generally don't want to call your target on the phone, but sometimes it can yield results too; it often depends on pure luck and whether you already know the right person to call (and whether or not the receptionist has been programmed to deflect all cold calls). But know that if you call the wrong person, you will not find out who the right one is. And knowing how hit-or-miss it can be, I can't recommend pure *chutzpah* as a way to open the door.

Keep in mind that editors run on schedules

Monthly magazines generally work on a four-week cycle (12 issues a year plus a 13th "holiday" issue is common), so if you call or email on a Friday and don't hear back, you might have caught them on a crunch week. Try again in two weeks and you might have more luck. For online publications, maybe 3pm is the worst time to call, and you don't realize it; try in the morning next time. And you never know when someone is temporarily away on business.

Being obsessed with hearing back will backfire; one eager beaver recently bugged one of our editors to the tune of at least one message a day. For his rampant enthusiasm, he got added to the spam filter and his phone messages were deleted instantly.

I was one of those eager beavers, and I paid the price myself. I submitted writing samples to *Entertainment Weekly* in the mid-'90s and did not hear back, so I called about a week later and left a message on the section editor's voice mail. I didn't hear back, so I would keep leaving polite, short messages every 10 days or so. I resubmitted my samples after a few more weeks, and always left between 10 and 14 days before trying to contact the editor again. Nine very long months later, he called and said no thank you, but he'd keep my work on file. (This usually means "I threw it away, and you are not getting work." Not always, but at least it's polite.) I stopped pitching. And that's the real reason he called me—to get me to go away.

Know when to give up

Clearly, I pushed it too far with *EW*—they called me not out of respect, but out of a desire to stop me from calling. I burned that potential bridge through sheer annoyance. Nobody's going to hire a writer who crosses the line from persistence to harassment, and if they remember your name in a case like that, it will be in a negative context. Some outlets simply won't want to hire you or may not be hiring anybody when you happen to contact them. A refresher packet with another polite re-introduction and your latest, greatest clips six months down the road is much more appropriate.

This is a lot of information, but it really boils down to approaching the outlet in a professional manner—knowing what your role will be to the existing staff and appreciating what their roles and responsibilities are to the publication. If you do manage to catch their attention, it will only matter if they see you as a valuable addition to their team.

"So How Did You Get Noticed?"

True confessions time: You know how I just said not to cold-call an editor to get their attention? That actually paid off for me. Starting out as a music journalist, I landed my first big gig at *Guitar World* because I phoned up the editor-in-chief and asked if he'd gotten the résumé and writing samples I'd sent the week before. He said he was busy running a magazine and didn't have time to read all of the mail; what did I want? When I said "freelance work," we chatted for a very few minutes, and he asked me to come in the next day for my first test assignment.

I wound up working at that company for three years.

I got *extremely* lucky. The timing was right and, somehow, my straightforward tactics did not offend him. They would probably annoy the hell out of me if someone tried it on me today. I've since talked to that editor and asked why he gave me the time of day. He said giving passionate newbies a shot was just part of his personal management style, and he admits he is in the minority in this regard. Tactics like that shouldn't normally work and probably won't. It's better to be professional and informed instead.

THE GUY WHO TALKED HIMSELF OUT OF A JOB
A tale of emotion, drama, and blogging

Before we go any further, I want to bring up an anecdote of how *not* to present yourself to potential employers. This isn't strictly a tale about freelancing, but seeing as how you are going to be trading on your writing skills, it's definitely relevant now that we're getting serious about how you will be approaching professional publications. What's more, it's better you read it here and now than in an anonymous email in a few months.

I joined the U.S. team of GamesRadar.com very early on—I was editorial employee #2, hired after the site's editorial director had come over from the U.K. to head up the project almost a year before the site actually launched. Because I had the time and the experience, I helped go through the resumes and writing samples for the people who'd applied for the open editorial positions. There was actually an embarrassingly large gap between the time that the jobs were posted and the time that people got a reply—like, five months—because so much of the site was being conceptualized in the meantime. The call for editors simply went out too early. By the time we contacted people, they were all surprised to find we were still interested. I don't blame them.

Part of the candidate-screening process was left up to me. I was asked to check the résumés out, read their writing samples, look the people up online, and see what else they'd written. This is a standard procedure; a Google search can show you a lot of a freelancer's work in a hurry, including the stuff they didn't include with their résumé. It might not be as polished, but that's just as important to see if you're looking to hire them.

In my short list was a guy whose name was…well, let's call him Crash, because that's what's going to happen to him.

Crash had good writing samples but not much professional experience. Armed with his real name, I was able to find his personal blog, where he often talked about how he didn't like his part-time job and had loftier ambitions. One older post even noted that he was applying for a job at a new gaming website, but then was sad that he didn't hear back. Because he also used the same online nickname in several gaming forum communities, I found some of his forum posts, which talked about his goal to set up his own editorial website. Crash was young and eager and had a bit of an attitude—something our editorial director liked, as he wanted to establish GamesRadar's voice as snarky and challenging. So Crash was one of only about a dozen people contacted for an interview. After having read his blog, I thought this was the coolest thing that could have happened to him. He'd gotten noticed; he was about to get his shot at writing about games full-time.

Here's where everything goes horribly wrong. I checked Crash's blog the next day, and it was filled with all manner of delusional things. He boasted that he had gotten a call back from us, and that this was clearly proof that we recognized his brilliance. We must have figured out that, as he already knew, most of our publications were pieces o' crap and that we needed his help if we were ever going to make something good. We had obviously realized that we were idiots to have turned him down so many months ago and that the only reason we'd be calling him this late is if we were desperate for what he alone could give us—and that he intended to leverage that advantage to a big paycheck and a lot of editorial control. He was going to make us pay for how we mistreated him by taking the job and showing us how it should be done. I mean, he had a whole revenge fantasy scenario worked out; in his mind, he'd already gotten the job and taken over the site. I guess he had forgotten that he was applying for an associate editor position and would be one step above intern in the editorial hierarchy. Also, he still had to impress us in person, and we hadn't even met.

So I mentioned this blog post to the editorial director, who would be conducting the interview, just as a point of conversation— "Hey, you should be ready for this guy when he comes in." And when the editorial director read the post for himself, he exploded in a string of vulgarity that I believe only British people can get away with spewing. No way was this arrogant kid going to set foot in the office, I was told. The editorial director immediately stormed over to the HR department, which sent a much more polite email to Crash, saying his interview was canceled and when we were ready to reschedule, we would call him. The email did not reveal why the interview was being canceled.

This is life in the Internet age—the reality of living on Facebook, of posting your thoughts on a blog, of trying to get attention (and then ultimately get paid) for your viewpoint. This is good, and I do encourage you to use sites and services like Twitter, Facebook, LinkedIn, Google+, and WordPress to create some visibility for yourself—they're all fantastic ways to connect with potential employers. But you are a writer, so as a result, *anything* you write can and will be used to define you. It does not matter where you post it or whether you consider it to be off-limits or not. Your writing, in any form, is *always* a reflection of you. Be mindful of what you say and how you say it. A hiring editor, freelance or full-time, is very likely reading everything you choose to say, so your last blog post could well be your first impression.

HOW FREELANCING WORKS
Surprise! There are rules, so you should know them going in

The good part about being a freelancer is that you are in charge of everything. That's also the bad part. Nobody's telling you how to do your job, so if you want to scribble unintelligible notes while beating bosses at three in the morning, have fun. But nobody's telling you what you need to do your job, either. If you're a freelancer looking for professional work, it's often assumed that you already know what you're doing and already have the necessary equipment on hand, as well as a detailed knowledge of the procedure. Uh, no.

So, before you go charging into the wild world of mercenary writing, here's what you'll wind up getting (and giving) to do it right.

An assignment letter
Unfortunately, you can't say "I'll just write a review of this new game I just rented and send it into the magazine/website, and if

they like it, they'll print it." You need to have an agreement ahead of time with the outlet that will be printing your work. In most cases, when you get an assignment from an editor, they'll supply you with a piece of paper or an email that says what you're doing, when it's due, how many words it should be, and how much they intend to pay you. This may or may not also include the listing of a *kill fee*, which is what you get paid if they accept but don't run the article. You may have done an awesome job, but the publication might have to cut your review in favor of some breaking news, and it won't be fresh next issue. If they didn't use it, but you held up your end of the bargain, the compromise is a kill fee, so you still get a little cash for your effort. Kill fees vary by publication, but are usually between 1/3 and 1/2 of the original agreed fee. It's worth asking if a kill-fee system exists when you get your assignment letter.

A confidentiality agreement

What you are about to witness is secret. The publication is held accountable for this, and a combination of ethics and legal threats keeps them from talking about games in development before they should. Naturally, if you're going to see or evaluate games before they're released to the general public, you'll need to be held accountable, too. Many pubs will ask you to sign a scary piece of legal paperwork. Some just call it a freelancer agreement, others use the industry standard term of *non-disclosure agreement*, commonly referred to as an *NDA*. You should read these before you sign them—they basically say "You can't talk about this to anybody"—but you *will* have to sign them. They are for everyone's protection, including that of your kneecaps. Sign it once, and they'll keep it on file.

Speaking of legal paperwork, you may also have to fill out a W-9 tax form, which is another sign-once-and-forget-it necessity of getting paid for writing. Remember to declare these earnings by

April 15, because your employer will. If you wind up doing a lot of freelancing, you may have to worry about self-employment tax; look up Schedule C and ask your favorite math nerd for help.

Reviewable code

What do you call a game before it's a game? It's reviewable code. These go by many names—a gold disc, a silver disc, a build, a beta, a final, a reviewable, or some combination of those terms. We'll get into details on what you need to use them in the next segment. But unless you are being asked to rent a title on your own, you'll be getting the game in some form from the editor who assigned you the review.

They'll want it back when you're done reviewing it, so take care of it and show it to no one, ever. Especially those friends you're trying to impress. Secret, remember? If you need to test the multiplayer aspects, don't just invite your pals over. Contact your editor, and they will request a session with the game company's dev or QA team. Also, it's perfectly fine to ask your editor for their FedEx number or otherwise get them to pay for return shipping. Busy editors may not remember to ask for games back, but they want them back, and will respect—and employ—you more if you take care of this grunt work like the professional independent contractor you are.

What's more, editors are accountable for that pre-release software, to the point where it's fingerprinted to them—if someone copies it, they also copy that invisible digital fingerprint that says "we gave this particular copy of *Alien Shot II* to *Official Game Critics* for review." So if it goes missing under your care…we're talking huge trouble. Lawsuit trouble. Federal agents at the door trouble, and I'm not exaggerating. There have been cases where pirate copies of software have been traced back to the reviewable code supplied to editorial outlets. In at least one case I can think of, editorial offices were searched, and items were seized. Do *not* risk it.

Game documentation

Generally, reviewable code comes with some sort of fact sheet,
a draft of the manual, or a cover letter identifying what it is.
Occasionally for adventure games, you'll get a walkthrough for the
first few levels to get you off to a good start on a long game. But
the fact sheet is gold, as it contains stuff like the number of levels in
the game, the ESRB rating, the street price…all that little info that
you need to fill out a review template so the reader will have all the
consumer information they need. If your editor doesn't give you a
fact sheet or a copy of the instruction manual, ask; they might not
have gotten one, but they might have simply forgotten to include it,
or they can send you a quick email with the facts you need to write
the rest of the piece.

An invoice

Everything else on this list has been sent by the editor to you; this is
what you add to the packet when you send it all back. You do want
to get paid, right?

After you've finished and submitted the assignment, you are
due to be paid the amount specified in the assignment letter—yay,
money! You won't get it right away; it'll take several weeks for your
invoice to be submitted, approved, added to the company's pay
schedule, and then mailed back to you. To make matters slower,
many places pay on publication, which means your invoice doesn't
even go to the accounting department until the article is live on the
site or until the magazine starts showing up on newsstands and in
mailboxes. A standard term to know is *net 30*, which means you are
due the money 30 days after the invoice is submitted.

There is no universal form for an invoice. Ask your editor if
they have a preferred style, but if they don't, all invoices contain
the same elements: Name, address, phone number, Social Security

number, a brief one-line description of what you did to earn the cash (mention the issue or article's publicaton date, the game title or name of the article, and its length in either word count or page fraction, if the editor told you), assigning editor, outlet, any billing codes you've been given, and the amount promised as payment from the assignment letter. It's worth putting "net 30" down there somewhere too. Collect all that in an orderly fashion in an email or Word document and send it as an attachment or a printout. Then you wait. And then you cash the check and blow it all on the next big game preorder.

GAME GEAR

To be a successful freelancer, you'll need the tools of the trade. Trouble is, you may not be able to get them.

Freelancers are essentially small businesses with one employee. You reap all the profit, but you also have to lay out for all the expenses. And it's sad to say, but some of the best things in life are not free— you'll need some basic gear before you take on this job.

Development hardware

This is less of a mystery when it comes to online publications, but one of the great paradoxes of game review is how a game can hit store shelves in December while a review of that game also appears in the December issue of a print magazine. A magazine is created over several weeks, what with all that writing, page designing, proofreading, printing, shipping, mailing, etc. So if the game is not ready for release, how can someone review it? And if the game is ready for review six weeks before it comes out in stores, why don't they just put it out so you can buy it as soon as possible?

The answers are certification and special consoles. It takes between nine and 18 months (if not much longer) for a game to be created; the last few weeks or months of that process are usually dedicated to polish, bug-testing, proofreading and, when all those steps are done and the game is finished, the all-important certification. If a game is made for release on, for example, Xbox 360, Microsoft gets to approve it before it's released (and the publisher pays for the privilege of putting it out with Microsoft's blessing— Sony and Nintendo enjoy similarly lucrative approval processes). That certification process takes around six weeks—Microsoft will put it through its paces, make sure the content is something they want to be associated with, make sure the game is high enough quality to be released—but for all intents and purposes, the game is done and expected to pass. In order to get a review into magazines around the same time as the game hits shelves, publishers often supply "release candidates" (RCs) or "final gold discs" to those print publications who have a long *lead time* (the amount of time it takes for a magazine to be created and show up on newsstands). It can be anywhere from three to eight weeks, depending on the publication. Online publications will often get a pre-release review copy after the product has passed certification; they might get a final retail copy a week early, but they're just as likely to be reviewing 100% final code from a gold disc.

To run these pre-release versions of the games, you need special hardware; your garden-variety, bought-it-at-the-mall Xbox 360 won't recognize these official homemade discs because part of the certification process is the addition of a security measure so that only games Microsoft has approved will run. To run the pre-release code, you need a custom-made game console to do it. These are commonly called "demo kits," "test kits," "dev kits," or "debugs," and they are usually slightly physically different on the outside:

development GameCubes were teal while original Xbox debugs (which actually said "Xbox Debug" on the front) were translucent green. Sony makes the Test versions of the PS2 and PS3, with the word "TEST" in capital letters where you would normally find the PS2 logo and just below the PlayStation 3 logo. And if you want to run beta software, you need the hardware to match.

The thing is…if you don't already have access to a debug, you probably won't be able to get it. These are not machines you can buy off the rack (developers have to buy them, and they're about 10 times more expensive than the consumer versions), and they're not the kinds of things that Sony, Nintendo, and Microsoft tend to hand out to anybody who wants them. As a new freelancer, you won't get one of these. After a few years, you might have enough clout to request one, and even then, it's on a loaner basis—the company will ask you to sign some scary paperwork, and they have the right to revoke your use of that debug system at any time. That's all well and good, but that doesn't help you right now.

Depending on the assignment and your proximity to the publication's office, you might wind up getting one on loan from the magazine or website for the length of time that it takes you to do your review. Alternatively, you might have to go to their offices and use their equipment on-site. It's a hassle either way.

This causes a lot of pubs to not send this kind of work out to new writers. If it's a game that's already out on store shelves, something you can buy or rent, it's probably a low priority to be covered, and you might pick up an assignment to review it in case of emergency—like if the magazine needs something to fill a third of a page at the last minute if something drops out. Online, it's a different deal; you may be able to rent recent games and help fill out a site's coverage in a timely fashion.

That doesn't mean there are no ways for you to review pre-release games, though. Handheld systems like the Nintendo DS will run pre-release software fine; the games arrive on large, reprogrammable cartridges that work like any other handheld software. Reviewing early versions of iOS games sometimes requires giving your iDevice's specific serial number (called the UDID; Google it, and you'll learn all you need to know), so the publisher can link the evaluation software to you and you alone. And of course, nobody's come up with a proprietary PC format—you can install a Windows, Linux, or Macintosh game for review on any home computer. So, if possible, you might want to pitch for those formats first.

Also, remember that the software you get will almost certainly be fingerprinted for security purposes. You'll need to uninstall the game and return the disc when you're finished, and it's not a bad idea to offer the editor your save files if possible. This is partly so they can use them to get screenshots if necessary, and partly to show that you really did dig deep into the game for the review.

Oh yeah, and a word processor

Most people use Microsoft Word as the standard word-processing software; it might have even come with your computer. If not and you can't afford the latest version of Microsoft Office, consider OpenOffice, free at openoffice.org. This is an open-source project—anybody with programming skills can help write the software. The word-processing component of OpenOffice, called Writer, reads MS Word documents and saves in a bunch of popular formats (including the handy universal rich-text format, commonly called RTF). It's available in multiple languages for multiple operating systems, and free is always a good price. I have edited the same documents while switching between OpenOffice and Word without any major issues.

Just don't use Notepad. We're not savages.

FROM SCREEN TO SCREENSHOT
How do you get screenshots, anyway?

Let's assume you have a review assignment for the PlayStation 3 version of *Alien Shot*. The publication's review guidelines say you're responsible for supplying your own screens. That makes sense; the images should match what you're talking about, so the readers can see what the game looks like for themselves, and they can see visual evidence that supports your opinions.

Once upon a time, strategy guides were created by staff artists *drawing what the levels looked like*. The technology for showing what they wanted to show was simply not there. For reviews, some magazines videotaped their consoles, then used still frames from that VHS video to create screenshots. Others just took photographs of TV screens. You can imagine how ugly that looked. And it still does look ugly, so if you were hoping to take high-res digital pictures of your HDTV, sorry, that won't work. No serious publication will run photos of your TV screen, unless they are chronicling some rare glitch or bug as part of a news story. You're going to need something more sophisticated.

There are two ways to get screenshots from a game: One is to ask the developer or publisher to supply them, and the other is to take them yourself. Because you won't have access to the developer or publisher directly, your editor will have to make that call, but many publications don't like to use the standard, canned shots provided to all publications anyway, so they prefer to take their own images. And when they assign work to outside writers, they often expect (or at least hope that) their freelancers will take their own screens. Some publications even pay a little extra for this because it's above and beyond simply writing words; some don't. Check with your assigning editor.

Folks lucky enough to have access to debug hardware sometimes have developer-level tools that let them get screens while they play, but most people—especially fledgling freelancers—will not have access to such luxuries. Unless you live near the assigning publication and can swing by to use their equipment, you're going to be literally left to your own devices. The explosion of "prosumer" digital video equipment, like personal video recorders (PVR) and fast data transfer standards like USB and FireWire, has certainly made turning video into stills a lot easier than it was even five years ago, let alone 10 or 20. With the advent of digital video, you don't lose much if any image definition—you can plug a game console's video cable into a camcorder or component cable into a high-definition PVR and get gorgeous video straight from the source. Then take that video into iMovie or Windows Media Player, and you might be surprised at how good a single frame looks.

However, it will probably cost you. One publisher of several magazines and websites invested roughly a quarter of a million bucks just into a fiber-optic storage network with computers and high-end capture cards so they could capture 720p games at 60 frames per second if they needed to. Guess what? They needed to. But realistically, you aren't going to have that kind of scratch. Some portable video cameras and recording decks will let you record HD game footage for a surprisingly affordable investment, so look for a PVR- or computer-based video capture equipment that features HDMI or component inputs and start your price shopping. (I am hesitant to mention specific gear, because this particular segment of the prosumer video market changes so rapidly. Seek and ye shall find web forums with lots of detail about the current hotness.)

For PC screenshots (and a handful of console games, like *Halo 3*), many games have snapshot functionality built in; just check your options menu to see if there's a screenshot button already assigned to some far-off key, like Print Screen or F12. Steam now assigns F12 as its default screenshot key, regardless of what game you are playing, and lets you review the screens after you've exited the game—a huge convenience. If you prefer to go it alone or need to take screens of websites as well (maybe your own work once it's published), there are third-party programs like the incredibly useful HyperSnap DX, which is particularly handy for taking game screens with Direct X layers and other advanced video tricks that confuse and confound lesser screenshot utilities. You can download the trial version from hyperionics.com; the paid version has been my screenshot program of choice for several years now. Another popular app in the PC gaming community is FRAPS, which gamers use to record footage of the games they're playing. It also takes stills (or you can export stills out of your FRAPS recordings) and it, too, has a free trial, but you'll need to pay the shareware fee to unlock it before you use it for professional screen-capture purposes. In other words, if you have a gaming PC, you already have the ultimate test bed for practicing your screenshot skills. Get crackin'.

That leaves handhelds. There's a screenshot function built into the iPhone and iPad (press the Home and Power buttons simultaneously) and the PS Vita (press the screen button and Home button simultaneously), but the Nintendo DS family of systems has no way to output its video signal beyond its twin screens. The pro publications use special dev kit hardware with high-end video-capture equipment, but you almost certainly won't have access to either of those tools, let alone both. Unfortunately, this means using screens provided by the publisher more often than not.

PC capture software, digital video devices, high-end video cards...it adds up cost-wise, and quickly. You have to think of it as a business expense and an investment. You need to be self-sufficient as a multiplatform freelancer, and having these tools is a major step in that process. You might not be able to get them all right away, but you'll probably need to get them all.

HIT THEM WITH YOUR BEST SHOTS
Now that you know how to take screenshots, how do you make them not suck?

When you're taking stills from games for review, you need to think like a photographer. You need to capture a moment in time, something that's visually pleasing, preferably memorable, that also tells part of your editorial story. Good luck!

It won't be hard to determine which moments make the best screens, if you're looking at the game critically. What made you go, "Wow!" when you saw it? Take that. What represents the visual style of the game? Take that, too. What screens have you seen that make you think, "I can't wait to see that in motion?" Bingo.

Shot composition—sense of balance to the image—is extremely important. You have to think like a photographer, shooting the virtual landscape, and let that image tell its own story within the borders of the frame. A magazine's art department may crop the screenshot to fit a layout or a template, but an online publication usually runs the full screen, for better or worse. So even if you've got an awesome crash in a racing game, it's not really as compelling if it's only showing something cool on half of the screen. There are exceptions to this rule that we'll get into shortly, but generally, you need to stay aware of where the action is taking place and keep moving around until you frame it for maximum balance and impact.

The dirty secret: Sometimes when you lose, you win. Many times, I have to die to get a really compelling screenshot. Blasting aliens is fun, but sometimes seeing that beast lunging at the camera while the edges of the screen frost over with crimson edges does a better job. Some folks think this is a good time to show off, and make the mistake of taking screens that make them look like a badass, like a long note streak in *Guitar Hero* or a full health bar in *Street Fighter IV*. But the reader wants to see what the game will look like when *they* are the badass; they're really not looking at your score or your performance. They're looking for a reason that they should check the game out for themselves. And facing danger is usually one of those escapist fantasies that screens illustrate. So show them some danger.

I'm going to use images from Epic Games' *Gears of War* to show some concrete examples of what I'm talking about—both the good and the bad. These are the same screens I used for my *Official Xbox Magazine* cover story review, so these are very real examples of screenshot decisions I had to make and how I made them.

©2006, Epic Games, Inc.

Gears of War is famous for its Lancer chainsaw / rifle hybrid, so showing the game's signature weapon is a priority in a review. This screen has some things going for it, but just enough wrong that I wouldn't use unless I absolutely had to. The blood splatter covers both characters' faces, the scene is off-center, and most crucially, you can't see the Lancer itself. You're basically letting the caption to this screenshot tell the story instead of the screen itself. It looked great in motion, but it just doesn't translate here.

©2006, Epic Games, Inc.

I like this one a lot more. Even though you still can't clearly see either character's face, it's very clear that whatever head this enemy has, it won't be attached for long. The Lancer is clearly visible, baring its chainsaw teeth, and player character Marcus Fenix is clearly controlling it. The splayed limb adds a sense of tension, and while this is also not centered, this image can be cropped easily, too.

©2006, Epic Games, Inc.

The cover system is another important element in *Gears of War* that you'll want to illustrate in your review. Unfortunately, this screen won't do it well; the debris from the incoming shot also obscures the enemy's face. There's action, but there's not enough information.

©2006, Epic Games, Inc.

This screen features less action, but far more information about the cover system, because the diagram at the bottom of the screen explains "oh, I can shift over to the car!" very clearly. The shot composition also feels more balanced, and the empty, shadowy street gives a glimpse of the game's gloomy atmosphere.

©2006, Epic Games, Inc.

Boss battles are cool, and this fight against a Berserker is no exception. You're usually so focused on not dying that it's tough to take good screens. This screen clearly states the name of the enemy, which is nice, but he's too far away to look menacing—and Marcus is just standing there, anyway.

©2006, Epic Games, Inc.

Much better. Now we see just why we should be scared, and we have a nice close-up of exactly what will be eating our face if we do not survive this showdown. I intentionally lured him over to the wall so the camera would force a zoom and cut most of my character out of the frame. Marcus' head obscures a little bit of the bottom of the screen, but it's worth it to get a clear, menacing shot of a detailed character model that the average player will not stop to savor.

©2006, Epic Games, Inc.

In this shot, the Hammer of Dawn looks badass, but the Berserker is so far away, you can't really see what it's obliterating. It's not a very dynamic screen either; you don't get the sense that this death laser from the sky is terribly powerful.

©2006, Epic Games, Inc.

Here's the companion to the bad shot, only done right. You still can't see the Berserker's face—not a bad thing if you want to avoid spoilers—but the glow from the Hammer is solid, there are sparks flying off the enemy's body, and his limbs are outstretched— we know at an instant that whatever that thing is, it is vaguely humanoid and does not like being fried from space. He's also dead center, so there's no guesswork about where the viewer should look for the most valuable information in the screenshot.

Where are we going?

©2006, Epic Games, Inc.

Cinemas can offer you some good images of your protagonist—they're good for variety when you have a lot of combat shots in an action game, and they give silent props to the art squad on the development team. However, this one says nothing. Marcus and Dom are visible, but they're not doing anything interesting or dynamic. What is the reader benefit for this screen? I can't find one.

We have a plan to end this war, once and for all.

©2006, Epic Games, Inc.

Here, Marcus and Dom are gods. They clearly just stepped off the chopper, but they're already good to go. The Lancer is clearly visible and looks menacing; the melodrama of the dialogue caption adds a nice touch. If you needed one screen to instantly tell the player what the setup for *Gears of War* was all about, it would be this one.

©2006, Epic Games, Inc.

This is a perfect example of not just getting the right scene, but the right frame of that scene. This is a cool setup; it's clear our heroes are taking cover from something, and we can just barely make it out down the walkway. We get some destruction and cool architecture too. Not a bad shot, but...

©2006, Epic Games, Inc.

...not as good as the one where our heroes fire back. Marcus' muzzle flash lights up the scene, making the scene look much more active and vital—not to mention the spent shells we can now see ejecting from his Hammerburst rifle. This is why you take a ton of screens and more than once at each opportunity—one of them simply might be clearly superior when you go back to review them.

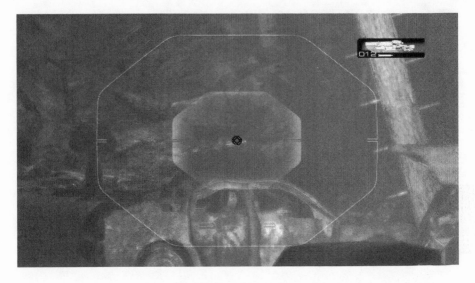

©2006, Epic Games, Inc.

Sniper shots are great—and ubiquitous—because they let you show something dynamic in close-up. This shot, however, does not. The red reticule at the center tells us we have a bead on our target, but what is it? There's just not enough detail or clarity in this frame to make it compelling.

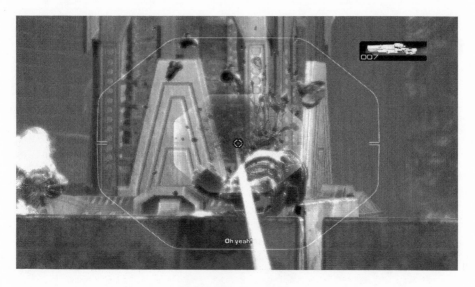

©2006, Epic Games, Inc.

Now *that* is compelling. Incoming shot trail, chunks of skull flying everywhere, and the gloopy mess left behind. A shot like this makes every gamer go, "Damn, I can't wait to shoot that gun." And that's the goal: Letting them vicariously feel cool through your gameplay experience.

©2006, Epic Games, Inc.

My rule of thumb is that a split-screen shot should always show a relationship between the player views—I want to show that these guys are in the same virtual space, playing the same game with or against each other. This Locust clearly has the drop on Baird here, but it's all potential and no payoff. As a result, all this image says is, "This game offers split-screen," and you need to say more than that.

©2006, Epic Games, Inc.

Six bullets later, and the relationship between these two panels is absolutely clear. Now it's the kind of kinetic moment that would have you and your friend howling if you were sharing a couch and causing this scene to happen. It conveys a lot more than just "Baird needs to watch his back."

©2006, Epic Games, Inc.

The splattery gore of *Gears of War* is distinctive—practically a character unto itself—and worth illustrating. But if you're not careful in how you choose your shot, you will instantly go from bloody awesome to bloody awful. Like here. I can't tell what the hell is going on, but I know it's messy. I'm sure it was a heck of a moment when the game was in motion, but this captured still is just slop and doesn't say anything of value to the reader.

©2006, Epic Games, Inc.

By contrast, this screen is arguably just as splattery but has much better shot composition. There's energy in both characters' body language, and the Lancer is clearly buried deep in Marcus' chest—the viewer knows what is causing this insane spray. The contrast between the ashen grays and the various crimson tones really gives this scene of bloody death incredible life. Remember what I said about losing to show danger? This is what I'm talking about.

Art for Art's Sake

When is a screenshot not a screenshot? When it's layout art. Sometimes the screens you take will be used in a different context— the art team might use it as a background image spread over two pages, or they might clip out a character or monster from your screen, isolate it, and run it as its own art element. It never hurts to take a few "beauty shots" that don't show gameplay, but do offer interesting character poses or say something about the game's atmosphere or art design.

Luckily, I married an art director. Katrin Auch can show you exactly what I'm talking about.

©2006, Epic Games, Inc.

I really like this shot. The body positions show a lot of tension, there's not so much blood that it obscures the focal point, and the stairs in the background give the scene some depth. Bummer that the composition is off, though, huh? Guess we'll have to crop it... unless the art team wants to use it as an opening spread for a feature story. All I did was write a headline, and Kat took it from there:

Other times, a screen might be used as character art. Many companies provide high-res renders of game characters, which can really jazz up a layout of rectangular screenshots. But when they're not provided, sometimes elements can be clipped out of screens and, if skillfully used, serve the same purpose. Take a screen where your character is isolated—full-body shots work best—and watch the color contrast between your character and your background. If the art team can't tell where a leg ends and a wall begins, take another screen. In games where you can't control the camera, stay alert during cinemas for interesting poses that can turn into portraits.

©2006, Epic Games, Inc.

If you think about other applications of your screens when you're taking them, you will give your art crew more options. They'll appreciate that you thought of their needs as well as your own.

Sometimes More Is More

When you're on assignment, always take more screens than you will likely need, then edit down to just the good ones before you send in your article. When I reviewed the original *Gears of War*, *OXM* ran about 30 screenshots from the 70 that Microsoft approved—but I'd taken about 1000. (I had no idea the duds would come in handy someday.) This also lets you offer your editor extra screens, so they have more options. If they ask for five screens, you can easily deliver eight or 10 good shots that show a variety of game elements, and you should provide captions for each screen. Just don't go crazy; too many shots is as bad as not enough (in general, more than three times what they requested is too much). But if you let your editor know that you have, say, several dozen alternate shots if they want them, you will look like someone who is willing to overdeliver on your assignments. In other words, a hard worker worth hiring again.

HOW TO GET FREE GAMES
You skipped straight to this section first, didn't you?

Everybody likes free stuff. There's no shame in it; free stuff rocks. But if you bought this book primarily to learn how to get free stuff from game companies, all I can say is…sucker! Greed is one of the absolute worst reasons to pursue this as a career, and games do not flow as freely as many people expect. You can score complimentary copies of a game with a legitimate reason, but it's not easy. That's by design.

Let's assume your intentions are pure, though. One of the first questions new writers ask is, "How do I get the games I'm supposed to review?" Well, you go through your editor. Your editor has a working business relationship with the public relations team at the game publisher, and that person sends them the confidential builds and final retail boxed product they need to cover the titles editorially. And "public relations" is something of an amusing phrase here, because if you are simply a member of the public, then they probably won't have a reason to relate to you at all. But let's say you are running your own website or you've been deputized with the job of getting new software for review on your own. You, Newbie Freelancer, must prove to the game publisher that you are serious about this and need their help (and their games) to do your job.

The keys to making this happen are professional communication and realistic expectations. Public relations associates are constantly inundated with unrealistic requests from greedy people. Anybody can pick up the phone, call the main number for a game company, ask for the media relations department, and introduce themselves. I've heard stories of optimistic youths telling the PR department that they're doing a school report on videogames and, um, they need one of every game the company publishes. Right. PR people ain't dumb, folks. Now, as a working freelancer, you may have a more legitimate reason to contact them and request product for review, but expect that you'll have to do better than simply calling and saying "gimme." Even if you do it politely.

There are two basic truths about asking for freebies:

Free games aren't free

You may not have to pay for them, but the company does. Most publishers stick to a budget of how many copies of games they send out; they have a certain number allocated for promotional use, but after that number is exceeded, they start getting billed by their own company. Remember, games are what make game companies money—you won't see automotive companies handing out new sedans to anybody who calls up and requests one. That four-door luxury family vehicle cost money to create, and they're going to need that car back, thank you. In fact, some companies may ask you for the boxed retail copies back; I've even mailed my review copies to other writers at other outlets at the publisher's request.

Some companies have a strict "one game, one publication" rule, and every so often, they audit that media list to see where they can save some money. If Bob Freelancer now works full-time for *Official Game Critics* and *Official Game Critics* is already on the list, Bob's individual listing goes away. That's justifiable, and it's not personal. It's just good business to manage your assets.

Public relations people expect results

Sending a game for review purposes costs a game company both time and money. Naturally, nobody's going to do that unless it's worth their while—namely, that you will not simply take that free game and play it with your friends, but will actually write and publish a review. That's not to say you have to write a *positive* review; you just have to write a review and see it published.

Every PR person must prove they helped get the company's latest products into the public eye. PR departments have to file weekly reports detailing what editorial coverage they assisted with this month—four pages in this magazine, a featured review on this site's homepage, a developer interview on this podcast, a 100-word review in a newspaper. Exposure is their business, and either you can help them get it or you can't. Calling and saying you are doing a story on the hot holiday releases is fine, but if they send you a stack of software, you will then have to prove to them that your story exists.

The easiest way to provide this proof this is to send a link or PDF file of the review once it's been published. I made a lot of friends by doing this early on without realizing it, because I did not know these reports even existed—I just thought, hey, you sent me a game for review, the least I can do in gratitude is prove to you that I didn't just take it and run. Little did I know that, by printing out and sending my online reviews to my PR contacts (because at the time, so few people were doing online game reviews that I often had to explain what America Online was), I was actually giving the PR teams exactly what they needed to prove that they were doing their jobs to their bosses. I was providing the exposure they needed, and I was giving them physical proof that they could insert directly into their reports. I didn't learn how helpful I had been until two years after I'd started doing it.

In case you haven't noticed, we're well into Catch-22 territory: You can't write reviews until you get the games, and you can't get games until you prove you write reviews. You're screwed, right?

The solution is easier than you think. Your first published reviews do not need to be based on pre-release games; they just have to be recent. Recent games are available at every software store on the planet, not to mention rental outlets. You can rent a copy of *Alien Shot* as easily as the next guy. Pitch a local paper on a review, and they may feel that a review of a game that hit stores just last week is plenty timely for their more casual games coverage. Ta-da—instant credibility! Now you can go to the *Alien Shot* PR folks with a copy of recent, relevant coverage and say "I know you also have *Hamster Ninja* coming out soon; could you send me information on that title?"

That's an important distinction: It's going to be easier to ask for information on games rather than the games themselves. Sending information is a no-risk option for PR; after all, they want people to know the game is coming out, so anybody who might be a valid press member should probably get the press releases. Ask to be added to the company's product announcement list so you get press releases direct from the publisher to your email box. Unlike the press releases you might read on the company's website, the ones sent out to a private media mailing list will include contact info, telling you exactly which PR agent is handling that title. Drop them a note or call them and request a review copy when they become available. If you really want to increase your chances, pitch a review of that title to your editor first; being "on assignment" will always carry more weight.

However, that's not foolproof. Your assigning editor may want to make that call themselves, in which case you'll have to accept it. Furthermore, creative would-be writers will often call a PR person and claim they are a freelancer on assignment for a publication when they aren't, just hoping to scam a freebie. As has been stated, PR folks are not stupid—they call that publication and say "Does this guy work for you?" This is not something to mess with—*at all*—because if you bluff a legit assignment, you will not only get busted, but you will be on that company's blacklist forever.

Eventually, if you follow up enough press releases with product requests and can consistently provide proof of coverage, you can ask to be put on the product list. It's a slow process, but remember—you're building contacts to last a career. This isn't about games, it's about relationships. And they take time.

Clearly, at this stage in your fledgling career, free games are not going to clog your mailbox. (Truth be told, they don't do that even in the later stages. Lots of editors place preorders for games they want, just like everybody else.) The best approach is to put yourself in the PR person's shoes. Know that they have to justify every free game they send out and that you can either help them or not. Your role is to make them look good at what they do. If you can do that—and you're going to have to accept that you'll be proving yourself slowly—you'll likely find that the process becomes easier over time.

The ABCs of Media Lists

The media is not just "the media"—some people are powerful, get cool promo items, are invited to press events, and are likely to get a call back right away, while other people are important but less powerful and less likely to be invited to events or sent fancy stuff. Most media lists often break down into three tiers.

The A list contains the most influential people at the most influential publications—the editor-in-chief, generally, or the editorial director. They get boxed games when they come in from manufacturing, plus they sometimes get nifty gifts or bits of swag that are sent to promote the awareness of a game. (This is its own animal with its own ethical issues, and it will be discussed later.)

The B list gets product and some of the gifts (t-shirts and messenger bags are the most common), but not the really fancy ones. Generally, if you're the main contact for a company on behalf of a publication or a really reliable freelancer who frequently works for major outlets, you'll find your way to the B list.

The C list gets information about the games, such as press releases and info sheets, but not boxed games unless requested. Usually the press release includes contact information so you know which PR person is shepherding that game and can get you more information or a copy of the game.

You start on the C list, which really does give you what you need to do your job. It's not as much fun as the other tiers, but hey, you're here to work, right? You can move up a tier by simply being a fixture in the industry; sometimes, simply repeatedly requesting boxed copies of games for review (and proving that you are covering them) is enough to bump you up to the B list.

What you don't want to do is ask to be upgraded. First of all, A, B, and C is just my terminology, so if you call someone and say, "Can I get on your B list?" they won't know what you're talking about. Second of all, if the company feels you're reliable and valuable, it will happen naturally; if you ask for it, you're doing so from greed, and you'll never get it.

However, you can earn your way up. Very good case in point, from Chris Kramer, who has handled public realtions for Sony Online, Capcom, and Konami: "I went to New York on press tour with Konami several years ago, and there was one guy who had a very small website. He came to our event, he was very nice, very polite, asked a couple of questions, very friendly. A few days later he sent me links to all of his stories, and he and I have communicated over the years ever since. He did everything right. He came in and said, "Hey, you don't know who I am, here's my website, here's what we're doing." He's always been proactive over the years; he lets me know when they are redesigning or changing the name. So I keep him on our contact database. He may not be the world's largest gaming outlet, but I know that he's consistent and he's doing it in a professional manner. There are lots of guys like that."

PUBLIC RELATIONS,
PERSONAL RELATIONSHIPS
Don't take my word for it—listen as the PR pros
tell you how to get on their good side.

One of the hardest things about freelancing is simply getting on the
map with the game companies. Consider how many publications
cover videogames. Not just the national magazines and big
websites, but city papers, fan sites, trade magazines, school papers.
Lots. And that means lots of people calling the public relations
department at GameCo, Inc.

Sometimes called media relations or media communications, PR
professionals are the game information gatekeepers. You might want
to get a hot new exclusive screenshot for *Alien Shot*, and they might
want to give it to you because they want you to be excited about
their next game. Whether you want to land an interview with the
developer for a feature or a Q&A sidebar, you need a spell-check on
the name of the boss that the developer mentioned in the interview,
or you are supposed to get an early build of the game as background

for your story, the PR pros are the ones you call. Respect their role, and they'll respect you.

But how do you know what's going on inside a PR person's head? How do you figure out what they need to get you what you need? Well…you ask them. I contacted a few industry veterans—some of whom work directly for the publisher, and some of whom handle PR for a publisher through an independent public relations agency—for their insight in hopes that they could explain their position in their own words.

The PR Pros

Lisa Fields
Roles: Public Relations Director, 505 Games; International PR Director, Activision
Helped launch: *Spider-Man, X-Men Legends, True Crime: Streets of LA, Transformers: The Game, James Bond 007: Quantum of Solace*

Chris Kramer
Roles: Senior Director, Forty-Seven Communications; Senior Director of Communications & Community, Capcom; Principal, Ronin Communications; Senior Director of Corporate Communications, Sony Online Entertainment
Helped launch: *Resident Evil, Silent Hill 2, Metal Gear Solid 2, Street Fighter IV, Okami, Resident Evil 4, Resident Evil 5, EverQuest II*

Abby Oliva
Roles: PR Director, Reverb Communications
Helped launch: *Guitar Hero, Rock Band* (all of them), *Deadly Premonition*

Matt Schlosberg

Roles: Vice President, cho HighWater Group; PR Manager, 2K
Games / Take-Two Interactive; PR Manager, Acclaim
Helped Launch: *The Dark Meadow, Prey, Sid Meier's Civilization IV,
Burnout, Burnout 2: Point of Impact, NBA Jam*

Robert Taylor

Roles: Senior Publicist, Activision; Assistant Account Executive,
Edelman Public Relations
Helped launch: Xbox 360, *Gears of War, Crackdown, Call of Duty 4:
Modern Warfare, Call of Duty: Modern Warfare 3*

How does someone get your contact info in the first place, and how do you prefer to be contacted?

Robert Taylor: Email is often the best way to get in contact with
people; that can often be found just by doing an Internet search and
figuring out who is in the PR department of a specific company.

Chris Kramer: Step one is to find the company's website. If you can't
go to a game company's website to find some way to contact the PR
group through a website, that company has failed in a spectacular
fashion—their website sucks. If you go to capcom.com and can't
figure out how to get to the press center, you shouldn't be doing this
job—you should focus on finishing seventh grade.

Matt Schlosberg: Definitely the best way to contact me for the first
time is over email if you're a freelancer. On email you can show
me some substance without taking up a lot of time. Sometimes I'll
get calls from writers, and they'll want to go on and on about what

they're trying to do and try too hard to make a good first impression. This will just make me want to get off the phone that much quicker. Just like magazine editors, we don't always have time to chit-chat on the phone; we need concise emails that get to the point.

Abby Oliva: Email is the best way to reach out to a PR person. If you can't find their email address, go to their company's website and look for a generic email contact or a main phone number. You can also look up a recent press release regarding a specific title—a media contact is *always* listed on a press release.

Robert Taylor: I don't mind being contacted cold via phone; the best way to do that is to call the main line and ask for the PR department. People then may be transferred to an administrative assistant who will determine who the call should go to. People calling in should make sure that they know specifically what they want before they call.

Abby: I would say don't call unless you already have a relationship established. While it seems calls might be more personable, you never know if it's a good time. And cold calls or introductory calls take time—you have to explain who you are, what you're doing, why you're calling—and honestly, I bet half the publicists you call don't even catch the first half of your conversation. That's why you might commonly hear half way through the call, "What did you say your name was again and what outlet are you with?" We're all busy, you included; introductory calls are tough. Start with an email.

Once they've found a way to reach you, what does a freelancer need to do to be taken seriously? What should they do to get and keep your attention?

Matt: A well-written email listing the writer's intent and indicating which outlets will be secured if I supply them with the information and assets they needs. Producing tear sheets and proof of their past work is a very strong way of grabbing my attention as well.

Lisa Fields: It's helpful to answer all of the publicist's potential questions up front before he or she can ask them: Who you are, what type of information/assets you are looking for, what type of story are you writing, where and when the story will appear, and what the deadline is. Many freelancers contact publicists demanding things; that's an automatic turn-off.

Abby: Email me. And if you don't hear back from me in 48 hours, email me again. Don't take it personally if it takes a while to get a response; we get hundreds and hundreds of emails every day. They back up and sometimes get overlooked. But when you are persistent, I will remember you. However, when you send your email, don't write a novel. Make it short and sweet: Tell me who you are, what outlet you work for or if you freelance, and tell me what you need. Do you want to be added to our media list so you receive news and press releases about our clients? Are you looking for a review copy for a particular game? Be specific.

Robert Taylor: Depending on what the time crunch is like, I may not get right back to someone, but I always try to at least acknowledge that I received their note. If they are requesting product, it helps if they include an electronic version of previously published work or links where we can find their stuff. If they are requesting an interview or comment, then it helps to provide previous links as well as sample questions.

Chris Kramer: People have sent me clippings of their articles in their local or college newspapers, or regional magazines. Those people I will end up putting on product lists. Because if someone is serious enough about their job to clip their stuff out of a paper, put it in an envelope, write a little note, include their contact information, and mail that to me, I'm thinking, "This person is doing a job. This isn't somebody who just wants free games or is just taking up cycles."

Abby: Once you've made contact and we've exchanged emails, add me to your IM buddy list. IMing or pinging a publicist is a great way to get in touch if your emails are going unanswered.

A zillion people contact you asking for games. Why don't you send them?

Lisa: There could be several reasons. If someone asks for a game on behalf of a media outlet I have never heard of, I'm going to need more information before I send it. Also, if someone just wants a game "for their library" but has no plans to cover it, I don't send them a game!

Matt: Another reason could be that the game they want to review is just not timely anymore. If we've shipped a game three months prior to the request, it doesn't do us any good to have another random review hit so much later.

Robert: Most people request a game the week it comes out. That's fine, but there is often a limited supply of games, and they go out very quickly. If you want to make sure to get on the early list, email the PR people a month or so in advance. If not, then prepare to wait a week or two at least until more product becomes available.

Chris: I don't send games if I have no idea who they are or what they're going to do with it. A lot of people who start up their own websites and want to start writing about videogames do it because they think, "Hey man, I can get games for free." And a lot of the bigger companies will do that—I've got about 2500 contacts in my database, so imagine what EA has, or Microsoft, or Sony. Fortunately those guys are so big that they can afford to send a lot of product out to a lot of places. We try to keep a tighter rein on the amount of product we send out.

So "free games" don't really exist?

Lisa: There is no such thing as "free" games, even for PR people. We have to pay for the copies we provide to the media. Those games incur costs from being manufactured, packaged, distributed, and shipped.

Robert: We do have to pay for games that we send out, and that usually comes from a PR budget. If you just have the boxed copy of the game and are sending it overnight, $20 is a good estimate. If you include a shirt or promotional item, that price goes up.

Chris: It's probably closer to $40, between buying the game, paying a royalty to first-party—first parties don't say, "Oh, you're sending these to the media? Okay, they're free." So we've got to pay for shipping, we've got to pay for someone to put all this stuff together in boxes, and then the time that it takes to put it all together. So it's probably somewhere between $35 and $40 per person, depending on platform.

Matt: I hate to say it, but there are some outlets that just aren't worth the expense. These are small fan sites that nobody has ever heard of. Sure, a guy and a few of his friends might read it, but does this give it any credibility, or get enough eyes on it to prove effective? It's not like we're sending out a new candy bar that costs a few cents; we're sending out games that are worth $50 to $60, and we have to justify that expense.

Abby: Our clients—the game's publishers—only give us a certain number of review copies. Supplying review copies costs money, so the number of copies can fluctuate for every title and every publisher. That means the PR rep needs to prioritize the review requests—and most times the biggest or most influential outlets take the top spots on that list. Always ask for a review copy if you're interested in reviewing the game. You may not get a copy, but you won't even get on the list if you don't ask.

How big does a publication have to be for you to send them product?

Chris: I need to make sure that every hour I spend doing media relations is going to get maximum exposure and maximum effect for that game. Where are the decision makers? Where are the eyeballs going? So if I'm not getting back to you, it's not because I hate you or don't like you or I'm a jerk—it's because I need to make sure that my time during the day is being focused to get the best return on investment for the coverage of my titles.

Lisa: Rather than a publication's size, I look at their influence and how they are a part of reaching the audience I am trying to reach. For instance, if I'm launching a game that appeals to tween girls, I'm going to find the most influential media outlets that will reach those girls, whether they are small websites or high-circulation magazines.

Chris: At the end of the day, unless you are Microsoft, Sony, or EA, you don't have an army of PR people. If you're Capcom, Namco, whoever, you have maybe two, three, five people in your PR department; there's no way you can keep up with everybody out there who is writing about games. We get hit from weekly newspapers from towns all across the country. The *Toledo Blade* just sent me an email that said, "How come I have not been getting games from you lately?" Because…I don't live in Toledo. Remind me, and I'll send you product. I don't have anything against the *Toledo Blade*, but I'm not sitting at my desk thinking "I wonder what they think about *Street Fighter IV* in Toledo?" Ultimately, I'll be like, hell yeah, let's get the *Toledo Blade Street Fighter IV*—but they're not top of mind.

What do you expect from a freelancer on assignment?

Matt: I expect honesty. I expect to know which outlets you're working with, what issue you're pitching them for inclusion in, what are the realistic assets that you'll need, and what are the realistic deadlines that you need to hit. Let me know that it's worth my time to work on getting you what you need instead of going directly to the outlet that hired you.

Abby: We have an obligation to our clients to secure coverage. Be extremely honest and specific with what outlet you're writing the story for, the intention or focus of the story, and let us know if the story has already been pitched and approved by that outlet's editor. Also, if you are working on a deadline, you need to let us know right away. Whether your deadline is two weeks away or within the hour, be specific about what you need and when you need it.

Chris: Generally if it's somebody coming out of the blue saying, "I'm freelancing for Outlet X" that you have actually heard of, what I'd do is reply back and say, "Hey, we don't send materials directly to freelancers; we send material directly to our point of contact at that outlet, and it's up to that person at that outlet to assign where that material goes." Otherwise I might have five freelancers who freelance for *Official Xbox Magazine* all hitting me up, all saying they are going to write the preview for *Resident Evil 5*…no. It goes to Dan at *OXM*. Dan's going to figure out who's going to write the preview for *Resident Evil 5*. It might *be* Dan. Freelancers…you're reviewing *Spongebob Squarepants: Battle for Bikini Bottom*. So we usually say, "Hey, this has to be assigned through your editor," but the really smart thing for that freelancer to do is to send a follow-up email after the thing runs saying, "Here's a link to my article where I raved about how awesome this game is," or, "Well, I was kind of hard on this game but I feel it was fair." Some sort of follow-up so we can see that this isn't a person coming from nowhere.

Abby: If you want to go above and beyond, send a link to your story or a PDF copy of your story to the publicist when it goes live. I always remember the editors who do that, and it's a great way to build a relationship.

Robert: The working relationship with freelancers doesn't begin and end with sending the game. We want to see what they thought; if they have any questions or need clarification, we are happy to provide that. We want them to succeed because that is one more person that will help us do our job of getting the product to the audience.

Abby: Also, it's not always the freelancers coming to us; more often, it's us coming to them asking if they're interested in a story that we'd like to see. If that's the case, I expect the freelancer to be honest and up-front. If I'm pitching you a story that you don't think has wheels, don't beat around the bush, tell me! On the other hand, if you like the story and want to run with it, communicate what outlets you'd like to pitch or what you would need from the publicist in order to help your chances of getting it approved.

By comparison, what do you expect from a staff writer or editor?

Abby: There aren't many differences here from those expectations of a freelancer; the biggest difference is that I already know where the coverage will appear, and if a staff writer or editor is reaching out to me, I'm pretty confident that we will see the coverage materialize. In that case, I expect them to tell me the focus of the story, what they need from me, when they need it by, and the tentative timing for the piece.

Matt: Pretty much the same exact thing that I expect from any freelancer. A journalist is a journalist; some just go about making their money and getting themselves published a little differently. The best thing you can do is be honest with me. If you don't think one of my games will make your next issue/show/web update, just tell me. If you need some exclusive screens, don't ask me for 10 if you're only going to use three. Things like that just waste people's time. I don't need to bug my developers to get me more assets and answer more interviews if they're never going to run. This gets them angry at me and makes me angry at the editor...nobody ends up happy.

Lisa: I don't think game reviewers know how much work goes into something as innocuous as sending out screenshots.

Robert: I expect to talk to a staff writer or editor a bit more often, as there are more opportunities throughout the game's lifecycle for interviews and previews and so forth. But I tend to expect the same thing from a staff writer or editor as I would a freelancer.

What do your bosses expect from you?

Matt: The world.

Abby: The world! Isn't that what all bosses expect? It doesn't matter if you're a writer or a publicist: Every boss needs you to produce, and at a PR agency, our bosses are the publishers and developers.

Matt: It's our job to make sure our company is presented in the most positive light possible to the public. We're the gatekeepers: We decide what information is released at specified points throughout the PR process, and we make sure the interest in one of our titles reaches its peak at launch. It's up to the developers to make the game good, but it's our job to make people know that it's good.

Chris: A PR person's job is usually judged on how many people have seen this game or heard about this game, to get the widest possible exposure for their title—whether it's a newspaper, magazine, website, on a blog, in a podcast, on a TV show, or whatever else we invent in the next 30 seconds. My philosophy is that our job is everything until we send a reviewable disc to the media. If at any point before a review happens, there's some sort of failure, then that is on PR—but from the point we hand you a gold disc and say, "This is reviewable, the game is out on this date," it's out of my hands.

Abby: At my agency, it's not about the number of stories you secure or how big those outlets are; it's about getting the *right* coverage with the *right* outlets for that specific game or product. It's about securing coverage that will ultimately sell through the title.

Print is not the dominant force it once was, but it still wields power in games media. Is there a fundamental difference in how you work with web and print outlets?

Robert: We have to be aware of the timing differential between the two, but we can do different types of stories with both web and print. Website front pages revolve quickly, but it's hard to do video in a magazine.

Abby: The detailed video features that the online outlets can produce often give readers a better perspective on your game. But at the same time, I still stare in awe at those graphically gorgeous print features. And since print publications have little space to dedicate to the sheer mass of titles, it feels great when your title makes the cut. I really like what some of the print outlets have done with their electronic versions for smartphones and tablets. It's almost like you get the best of both worlds.

Matt: In print, there are always creative new ways to deliver stories on games, but the bulk of coverage for a single game tends to hit as a news piece, interview, a first-look preview, a hands-on preview, and/or a review. Reason being, space constraints and frequency of coverage are much more defined in print than in online. With online, you can take a more detailed approach, breaking down features, creating unique video content, etc., all in an effort to continually roll out coverage on your title up until launch…keep the buzz going and the game in people's face. Online sites also have message boards, where people will discuss the game you're publicizing.

Lisa: Online is current; its reach is huge, and I think it's the best vehicle for viral campaigns. My only complaint about online is that the writing is not always up to par and fact-checking does not always happen. Print is ideal for exclusive in-depth, well-written features and showcasing artwork like screens and character renders.

Chris: From my perspective, a magazine cover is something that you get mounted and hang on the wall and pretty much forget about three months later. But online coverage is forever, because I will go and Google that whenever I want to find something out. So if someone screws up in a print preview, I'm like, "Oh well," but if they screw up in an online preview, I say, "Hey, you know what, that's 12 weapons, not 10; that's six levels, not two." Because that's going to live forever, and it's going to cloud the message eventually. Two months before release, all of a sudden, people are going to be like, "GamerHotDog.com said there only six levels; why are these guys saying it's nine? I only believe what GamerHotDog.com says." These days, in the 21st century, we are far more cognizant of what's happening online. Print is great for short-lived glory, and it's a great way to kick off a campaign, but ultimately, online is where it it's at.

What mistakes have you seen writers make that newbies should avoid?

Chris: The thing that irritates every PR person is the sense of entitlement that comes from some people.

Matt: Some writers think you owe them something, even if they are bad at their job, just because they happen to write for a living. There's this one freelancer who kept hounding me for early code to write reviews on our games. The problem was, I hadn't seen his byline show up in any of the outlets he claimed to write for in months. Plus, I had already supplied the code to the outlets he was trying to freelance for. Basically, he was giving me no reason to send him our games other than the fact that he wanted to play them. So I called a few of the outlets he said he was writing for. Two of these outlets denied ever even working with the writer, and two of them said that he hasn't turned in a story on time in over a year. Long story short, this guy has not and will not ever get anything from me unless the editor he's working for sends me an email explaining that he has been commissioned by them to write said piece.

Abby: One of the quickest ways to burn your bridge with a publicist is to tell them the focus of your story and then publish a story that focuses on something completely different. If you tell me the focus of your story, and that focus changes over the course of writing the story and going through other channels for editing, let me know. We agree to participate in stories when we know exactly what we expect out of them. It's almost like the publicist and the writer have come to an agreement of sorts. Our job requires us to attempt to manage tone and topic of coverage as much as we can, and there's nothing worse than me going to my client and telling them I've secured a story on topic A, and when the story publishes it's not at all about topic A and instead focuses on something completely different. For one, you screw over your relationship with the publicist. And sometimes, if it's bad enough, it's a good way to get a publicist fired.

Lisa: Don't be an event whore! There are many freelancers out there who get very insulted if they are not invited—or flown out—to events even though they have no plans to cover what is being shown at the event.

Robert: Don't be annoying. If you are not getting a response, send a reminder maybe once a week or once every two weeks—not every day!

Matt: There's nothing worse than getting an email from a writer that reads, "Hi, I'm a freelancer and I'd like to review one of your games. Can you please send me your latest release?" First of all, how do I know that you don't already write for an outlet that I've sent my latest game to? If it's already being covered, why would I waste an additional copy? Second of all, if you don't even know what game or games we're currently promoting, how do you know you can get your review placed? Basically, an email like this tells me that you're just some kid trying to get a free game. If you're professional, you have a plan, and you can produce results, then I'm all for working with you.

A TALE OF
TWITTER TERROR
A PR professional offers "a concrete example on how not to do things"

Gather 'round, kiddies—we're going to close out this section with a real-life horror story. I asked several PR professionals for their horror tales of working with the media—bad behavior, huge mistakes, stuff that up-and-comers should definitely learn from and avoid. One story stood out.

I have sworn to protect the identity of the teller of this terrifying true tale of how one editorial outlet not only shot themselves in the foot, but reloaded and kept pulling the trigger. Rather than try to summarize it, I'm going to let our mystery guest tell the story in their own words. Read and beware!

> We got contacted by a cheat code website. I guess they also do previews and reviews—awesome—but they're a cheat code site. They contacted us and said, "We haven't

been getting free games from you lately; we want free games." Pretty much phrased that way, too, but even more demanding.

We've been trying to control the amount of games we've been sending out because we've just been sending out tons of product and haven't been getting tons in return. A cheat code site is great, but that's not gonna do it for us. Us sending them games isn't going to get people to go, "Wow, I'm going to buy that game." People are going to go there to say, "I need to know how to make Lara Croft naked in *Tomb Raider: Extreme Backflipping*," or, "I need to unlock the rocket launcher in *Grand Theft Auto 5*." That's fine, I support that—but not with product.

So we wrote back and said, "Make sure you sign up on our press database, and you'll get all the information, but at this time, we're not going to be able to send you product." This led to—I'm not kidding you—a three-week series of phone calls and emails to my staff. And these weren't just like an email saying, "Hey, that's too bad, we'd really like to be accepted," they were, like, 500 and 600 word missives. "We're the biggest site on the Internet, we get more traffic than X, Y, and Z, you need to send us product, I can't believe you're treating us like this, la la la la la." They did that to two of my guys and then were phoning them. So now my guys are having their time taken up even more.

So finally I said, this is crazy, I gotta cut this off. I jumped in and sent a very nicely worded email to the person who runs the site, and said, "Look—we're very busy right now.

We've got a lot of things going on. We're launching two big games at the same time, and there are only *three* of us in PR. I need you to cool it. And I see you have already reviewed one of the games you're requesting; why are you asking for me for a free copy? Your review is already there. Fill out this questionnaire; we'll get back to you later. Please don't contact me again, as we are very busy right now, but I promise that we will come back sometime after we ship these products and things have calmed down." Very nicely worded, but in there I said, "We don't need any more calls or emails from you, we will evaluate once you fill out this form."

This, of course, led to a *1500-word email* back from this person. I just replied, "Fill out the form I sent you last time; I'll get back to you." I don't want to be a jerk; I'm not trying to be a jerk, but now this person is wasting my time, and even worse, they've pissed me off.

I already knew their website didn't fit what we were looking for in regards to support from an editorial standpoint, but I got their paperwork, and I filed it—we keep all these things from all these websites—and I wrote back, "We have a very well organized press center." We invite everybody to go there—big, small, *The Wall Street Journal*, BobTheGamer.com, it doesn't matter. You all have access to the same information and materials, screenshots, movies, artwork, fact sheets, press releases—anything you could possibly need to write about our games short of sitting down in a chair across from the producer is there. And that's our solution. We can't keep up with the entire Internet, but we want the internet to be able to keep up with us.

They finally cooled out and stopped sending us these huge emails about why they deserve product and how dare we treat them like this. So yesterday I got an email from the guy, and it was just a single line this time: "Hey, we sent you this form, and we haven't heard back from you." I could have just deleted that, but it's my job as a PR person to maintain contact, so I responded, "Thanks, we have your information. At this point in time, our product lists are closed. We will not be able to send you products right now, but things may change in the future, so make sure to keep up with us through our press site."

Now, I have TweetDeck open on my computer because I also run community stuff, so half my job is also doing outreach through the blog, Twittering, doing all this stuff directly to consumers. On TweetDeck, which is rad, I have a column that searches for any Twitter mention of my company. Two minutes after I sent this email, there's a tweet from this site that says, "From [the company]: 'We will not support you at this time.' WTF? We're the biggest website in the world. Let them know what you think."

This is *exactly* why we are not supporting this particular website, because they are not a professional organization—they're a bunch of Dudes on the Internet. They are probably getting great traffic for what they're doing; however, that is not the sort of behavior that I would expect to see from *The Wall Street Journal*, the *New York Times*, *Time* magazine, IGN, *GamePro*, GameSpot, *Official Xbox Magazine*...all these other outlets. And that's where I spend the majority of my time, because that's where the majority of viewers are.

So if you want free games and information from me, you need to act like the *New York Times*, not Dude on the Internet. Because Dude on the Internet can just go be Dude on the Internet—I don't need to interact with you, you don't need to interact with me, you can have your opinions, go for it, do it. I encourage people to go out and write and do this sort of stuff, because today's Dude on the Internet is tomorrow's editor-in-chief of GameSpot.

I think you can summarize it best as "don't be a dick."

LEVEL 3 GETTING IT

■LEVEL 4■

Keeping It

If you want to shift from independent freelancer to full-time staff member at a media outlet, you need to know a few things—like how to develop your editing skills, how to handle life in the spotlight, and yes, even how to dress. Look sharp!

WELCOME TO HAPPY HELL
You're hired! Now adjust your head space to office space.

As you step off the elevator, dressed in your absolute best t-shirt and jeans, you spot the logo right away on the frosted glass doors: *Official Game Critics*. The promised land. And now, finally, after so much hard work and perseverance, you work there.

The door is opened for you by a curvaceous woman wearing Lara Croft's famous tank top, shorts, and sly smile. As you pass through the hallowed entrance, you're immediately greeted by a man holding out two things for you to take—a stack of money and a six-pack of Mountain Dew. The smell of warm pizza fills the air as you are led to your office, which consists of a comfortable armchair encircled by large surround speakers. The chair is aimed directly at the largest high-definition television set is has ever been your pleasure to be stunned by. "Welcome," says the man, offering you another six-pack of Dew and backing away in a bowed posture of subservience.

Please, *please* tell me that you know I'm kidding.

Frankly, I'm not sure—I've heard some pretty interesting takes on what life is like behind the scenes at a videogame publication. The above is not too far off from what a lot of people believe it must be like to be an editor at a game media outlet. It's not even work! It's paradise! It's where I want to be buried!

Truth is, the real version of your average videogame editorial office is slightly less glamorous.(For one, they only give you one can of Mountain Dew.) Sure, there are toys on people's desks and cardboard cutouts of game characters from store displays, and other signs of a gleefully arrested development. But otherwise? Cubicles. Meeting rooms. Telephones. Pens. More cubicles. TPS reports.

So, I hate to be the bearer of bad news, but here are seven things that you will absolutely need to consider before you step through that office door. They may represent fundamental changes in the way you've been doing things as a freelancer.

Commuting

Your first challenge arrives before you do: How do you get to the office every day? If you have a car, you'll need to deal with traffic. In the San Francisco Bay Area, where many game publications, game publishers, and game developers have set up shop, traffic is a freakin' nightmare. Gas prices are through the roof, and one accident on a major bridge can leave you sitting in the car for literally hours.

Meanwhile, if you take public transit, you'll need to arrange your life around the bus or train schedule, and it might actually be more expensive than driving, as BART, the commuter train system in the Bay Area, can be. If you live close enough that you can ride your bike, you'll need to travel very light, which makes taking equipment like debugs home from the office a little painful. And if you wind up being able to walk to work, that's awesome, but rare.

Starting out, chances are good that you'll be living in an apartment, maybe one that you share with other people. That apartment's proximity to your office is a major factor—prioritize your apartment location and plan your commute accordingly. A cheap apartment far away from work may wind up costing you in the long run, because time spent (or rather, wasted) getting from point A to point B and back again can sap your good vibes and creative energy faster than you would ever imagine. I've lived 10 minutes from work and I've lived 60 minutes from work. Ten minutes is better.

Cubicles

Desks are a thing of the past; you'll have a workstation, which is like a desk, only not. Workstations are pre-fab, relatively-easy-to-assemble bits of particle board, foam, and metal that combine to make a small cage in the middle of an otherwise free-range space. A horizontal work surface is bolted to half-height walls, a swivel chair with a broken tilt adjustment is rolled up to meet it, and it's upon this slab of medium-density fiberboard that your computer will be placed. Now…make magic!

Actually, it's not that bad. Cubicles are one of those things people love to hate for what they represent more than what they actually are. But it's going to be your space, and you're going to have to learn to make it comfortable for you. This may take a little while, especially if you're used to writing in the privacy of your own home, where you can control the environment a lot more. If you don't have an office, you don't have a door, and if you don't have a door, you don't have true privacy. But you'll always have headphones, so learn to love them!

Exactly how you create a healthy, creative workspace will be different at every place you work because every place you work has different rules about how you can modify your workspace. Some offices let you put whatever you want on the pseudo-walls; others require you to have your decorations approved. I've seen everything from stark, sterile workspaces in beige and gray up through toy collections, Christmas lights, lava lamps, and rock posters crammed into an 8-foot-square box. Regardless, you're going to have to play the cards you're dealt. My dad worked as a computer programmer for 35 years and always adorned his office with a faux-cross-stitched sign that said "Cubicle Sweet Cubicle." 'Nuff said.

Your methods for making your cubicle both comfortable and creatively stimulating will vary, but there is no escaping the reality that anybody can "prairie dog" over your mini-walls and literally stick their nose into your business. This is amazingly distracting, especially when you are on deadline. You want to be a nice person and be social with your co-workers, but when Bob from Accounting needs a break, expect him to come over to your desk to take it and see what cool new games you're working on. That cardboard stand-up advertising the most recent Tony Hawk game that you strategically placed in your "doorway" with the cute word balloon coming out of Tony's mouth asking people not to disturb you won't actually do a thing to stop Bob.

Clothing

They do make the man, don't they? They also make an impression, and it's important to make a good one. You don't need a suit— c'mon, this is videogames! It's respectable, but not stuffy. But you might want to look into the term "business casual." Jeans are fine as long as they're clean and lack holes. Since so many game companies give away t-shirts to promote their titles, it's hard not to see someone wearing one. But having some polo shirts in your closet isn't a bad idea, because sometimes, you want to look at least vaguely business-like. And get some non-denim pants—khakis are fine. Honestly, you can get what you need to look "business casual" at Target, Walmart, or Old Navy, and you probably don't need to wear it every day. You just have to have it at the ready for days when it's appropriate. (More on this a little later.)

The important thing to remember is that people are watching you, whether you know it or not. The more outlandish you dress, the more immature you're assumed to be. Regardless of how well you write or how many deadlines you nail, some people will judge a book by its cover, and that bowling shirt with the flames all over it might actually come to define you in some people's minds. To them, even when you're just slaving away at your desk, you *always* represent the company…and they don't want you representing it looking like *that*.

Music

In an open cubicle environment, anything you say or play can be overheard. When you review a videogame in a cubicle, everybody has to hear you review it, too. Your office mates will tolerate that because it's part of the job, but they might not be so understanding if you want to play aggressive punk or hardcore rap while you work. When it comes to those times that you just want to crank your favorite inspirational tunes and get into your writing groove, you'll find you can't—it's just too distracting to inflict your jam on everybody around you. Take some of your new salary and get some comfortable, padded headphones that cover your entire ear. You'll need to seal in your music as well as block out the rest of the office.

Politics

We all like to think that when you're doing good work, people notice and will reward you for it. This is sometimes true, but the opposite is absolute fact: When you screw up, people notice. How long they remember and what other assumptions they make about you as a person and a co-worker fall under the tricky category of office politics.

Office politics is sort of like high school, only with higher stakes, because if the jocks don't like you in high school, they won't actively work to get you expelled. But if you make the wrong enemies on the job—by not respecting your spot on the food chain, not taking your responsibilities seriously, or by sheer ineptitude—that can have a very negative effect on your entire career path. Colossally bad impressions can go down on your permanent record and dog you for years as industry gossip as you move from job to job. It's ridiculously easy to become "that guy."

Navigating the waters of office politics is not easy. One day you might be really upset about something and blow off some emotional steam in a conversation in the hallway. Bam! The wrong person overhears and mentions to your boss that you have an unprofessional attitude or you're a drama queen. Push the review template's boundaries to the point where someone above you has to edit your work heavily, and pow! You've got a rep for not wanting to play by the rules for the good of the company. Make an off-color joke to friends while the president of the company happens to walk by? Thanks to those open cubicles, which let gossip and personal comments flow freely around the entire office, you just made your worst impression ever. Suddenly, that clever preview that you handed in early last week is discounted—"The new person does good work, *but*…" You don't want to create the idea that one day soon you will be more trouble than you are worth.

The main thing you can do on your own to avoid political problems in the office is to remember the chain of command. Let's say you're new at the company; you're eager, you're ambitious, you're happy to be living the dream. But you've got a supervisor who knows how things work, and that person has been charged with helping you learn the ropes and teaching you to be the best editor you can be. They should be your greatest ally, but they won't be if you start ignoring their advice outright, or turning to someone else, or talking about them behind their back. Things like that color how you are seen by others and how much faith they are willing to put in you.

Think of yourself as a commodity on the stock market: Before you buy a company's shares with your hard-earned money, you scrutinize all their products, see if you agree with their business methods, and look ahead to see the kinds of things that could happen in the future that would affect the situation. You'd do that if you were investing in a company; the same thing happens when a company invests in you.

If you're terrified by this point that you're going to have to learn to read minds and never speak to anybody about anything, relax. Not everybody is out to get you, and most people do not feel the need or desire to point out your every failure to anybody who will listen. But in those cases where you think that might be a danger—for reasons of jealousy, fear, cluelessness, or any one of a number of perfectly normal, perfectly catastrophic human emotions—a little paranoia and a lot of common sense will help you a lot.

Social skills

Some people are naturally charismatic; they're good with people, they're charming, they know how to say the right thing at the right time. Other people are dreadful at it. They don't know how to carry on a conversation, they don't put other people at ease when they try, and they seem to be wrapped up in their own little world. This is the kiss of death in an office environment.

We all know the stereotype: Gamers live at home with their parents, never see the sun, never leave their rooms or power down their game machines, and the closest thing they have to a real-life friend is a person on instant messenger of indeterminate gender and species named Neo94546, who may actually be a robot. Cruel and not so funny when it's applied to you, right? Problem is, if you can point out several examples, a stereotype ceases to be a stereotype and starts becoming an archetype. There *are* gamers who live like this, who have focused on their game knowledge and skills in a vacuum and are therefore unprepared for human interaction beyond waiting in line to pick up a preordered game. They would rather interact with fictional characters in a digital world where they have control—and who can blame them? It's much less messy. But even the most active guild on the most engaging MMO still leaves you unprepared for meatspace. The office? That's a real world. And you'll have to deal with it.

In your new job, you're going to attend meetings, and lots of them. There will be staff meetings, where you discuss ideas and split up responsibilities with your co-workers at the publication. You will host and attend game demos, where company representatives visit your office to show you the latest and greatest preview releases, or where you're invited to hop on a plane and interview a game's development team in its natural habitat. You'll be expected to call people on the phone to get and give information about when those new screenshots will be available and report on your publication's circulation numbers and/or site traffic. All of these will require above-average communication skills, verbal skills, and people skills. You're going to have to look people in the eye when you talk to them; you'll need to know how to discuss a topic and get to the point without rambling or mumbling; you'll need to listen when other people speak and be ready, when appropriate, to offer your opinion or suggestion in return. Compared to blasting aliens and saving princesses, it kinda sucks.

And this is to say nothing of your social relationships with fellow staff members. You will spend more time with your officemates every day than your family, so treat these people like family too. You will go to lunch together; you will survive crunch times together. Treat your staff members with respect and understand how your role complements theirs. Everybody is replaceable, but you will be amazed at the results when everybody treats each other as if they aren't.

It may take practice, but the office will not change its natural rhythms to match yours, so start polishing these social skills now. For a job where the word "videogame" shows up so prominently, literally 90% of your work will involve interaction with human beings.

Home? You have no home!

When you said, "I've always wanted to work at a media outlet," you probably didn't mean "I always want to be working at a media outlet, to the point where I never get to leave the office." Being an editor isn't a 24/7 job, but it can be, and there are times when you will find yourself at the office very late or working for the weekend out of sheer necessity.

This is not a 9-to-5 job. For one, most game editors don't like to get up that early. But in addition to your "normal working hours" in the office (the 40-hour-week is valid here), you will find that you sometimes have to take work home. You work when the work needs to be done. You've got a Monday deadline, but the game just arrived late Thursday? Well, then, that's what you're doing this weekend. The magazine pages have to ship tomorrow and there are still 30 to be proofread? Pack a lunch *and* a dinner. E3 is next week and your website has pledged to keep the news fresh every hour? Hope you saved some of that Mountain Dew from orientation. You may have heard tales of people sleeping under their desks when they were on tough deadlines; those stories are really true. That may seem excessive, but it's better than bothering to drive home at 3 in the morning when you know you just have to turn around and come back at 9 for a meeting.

The work week starts at 40 hours, but it can often creep into 60 and can even head into 70 and 80 hours during times of extreme pressure, such as the months before the winter holidays. That leaves little time for sleep and absolutely no time for goofing off or simply clearing your head. And the smaller your staff / the lower your freelance budget, the more work will fall upon you to complete. What's worse, such an overwhelming focus on your work makes it hard to build your social skills or get away from the office politics.

Pulling all-nighters for fun is one thing. Pulling them out of necessity makes them not fun at all. But sooner or later, you'll find yourself exhausted on the job.

These are all solvable problems, all things you can learn to minimize or simply learn to live with. Lots of really good writers have trouble transitioning to the role of an editor, and the seven things we just discussed are the main problems that trip them up. If you can plan for them, maybe they won't hurt so much when they happen to you.

THEY PROMOTE EDITORS, DON'T THEY?

The difference between writer and editor could be the difference between job and career

You've got your desk. You've got your computer. You've got your console. Do you have your socket wrench? If you see yourself as a writer, you might not. Wrenches are generally reserved for full-time editors.

Stick with me here.

What's the difference between a writer and an editor? In the game-review context, a writer creates something from nothing, explains their opinions completely, follows but finds freedom in the assignment's template, and hits their deadline. An editor does all of the above while fixing the mistakes of all the other writers—mistakes like failing to explain opinions completely, not following and not bothering to look for freedom in the template, and missing deadlines. Editors are the F1 mechanics of magazines; they find out what's causing the articles to run so rough, and when they find it, they fix it or remove it to optimize the piece for pure performance. Wrenches.

Things are going to go missing after the editor works on the document, but it's for the best. It might be a joke that the writer really liked but ultimately didn't work; maybe it was a pop culture reference that was too obscure. Slice! It's cut. It could be that the writer just went into too much detail about a small element of the game, and the review lost its focus in the process. Slash! Gone. It's the editor's responsibility to pare down and rework the copy as necessary, to get it ready for print. Sacrifices have to be made, and those sacrifices will, in accordance with Murphy's Law, be the writer's favorite words in the whole piece. The writer giveth, and the editor taketh away.

If that kind of revision to the writer's work sounds subjective, you're absolutely right. Some editors want to put their personal imprint on every piece of copy they see; other editors respect the original writer's voice to a fault, letting sloppy expression go under the auspice of "creative freedom." The best editors work somewhere in the middle, but still wield a lot of power. Editors don't have to come and tell you what they disliked about your work or even ask you for permission to change what you've written. They just do it, and you find out when it's published.

At videogame publications, staff-writer positions are hard to come by; take a look at any masthead, and you'll see mostly editor titles on the list and certainly all editorial titles up at the top. It only makes sense that the people with the most applicable skills will get the best and most permanent jobs. So if the power-trip aspect was not enough, the additional job stability should be ample evidence: An editor is what you want to be.

However, you simply might not be one. All editors are writers, but not all writers are editors. It's a different skill set, a more intense and responsibility-laden position, and everybody can't do it, at least not out of the box. Editors are the people who actually like spelling and consider grammar a complex but comforting friend. Editors take responsibility for the quality of the articles that appear in the final product, as well as all the other stuff discussed in the Know Your Masthead section. And worse yet, editors need to have good instincts to do their jobs well. How you did on the fake review test earlier in the book is a good indication for how close you are right now to being able to fulfill the duties of an editor and what you might yet need to learn. And being a reliable, responsible editor is the best possible way to move up the ranks at the publication.

The best way to acquire the skills of an editor is to be an apprentice to one. If you're just starting at a magazine or website, you might already have the title of editor without actually doing the applicable work. Express your interest to your supervisor or, if the publication has it, the copy chief or managing editor. Say you want to learn the ways of the Force and become a Jedi like your father. You'll likely be given an edit test (if you haven't been given one already) not unlike the *Alien Shot* review so they know how much you know.

From there, it's practice—working on lots of rough copy and having someone else analyze your analysis. But with enough practice, you can develop the necessary skills; you will be able to look at a review and go, "Oh, this is what's missing," or, "It doesn't say anything about this aspect," or even, "Hey, this is great, ship it." If it needs fixing, you'll have the tools to fix it immediately. With your wrench.

WRITING NOT-REVIEWS
Sooner or later, you're going to have to write something that doesn't have a score attached to it

This book is primarily focused on game reviews because they're usually the backbone of videogame publications. But obviously, there's more to it than that; you have to balance reviews with other articles, too. You already know that different editors have different responsibilities for different sections of the publication, and if you're on staff, chances are good that in short order, you will have your own subsection to look after as well. And you may not have a choice of what it is ("hey, someone needs to do this section that nobody else wants to do...and you're the new guy"). Any of the following could be your new domain to master.

News/lifestyle

Online, news is king, and it's the source of a lot of eyeballs for your media outlet. Being a news writer actually borders on real journalism. If you parrot a press release, you're just shooting yourself in the foot; nobody will want to read it, it tells the reader nothing new, and the reader (who, thanks to the web, also has access to the press release) knows just how lazy you really are. But if you get on the phone and ask questions and solicit quotes from the parties involved and do some research as to what your topic will mean to the reader, then the title of game journalist might be valid after all. But it's still something you have to earn. (And no, rumor-mongering does not count as "educated speculation.")

Many online outlets give their news writers a byline, but not all publications do. That might be a bummer for your ego, especially seeing as how news reporting is actual work, but the upshot is that, uncredited, you are now the voice of the publication. You get to sound authoritative and when people discuss your articles in casual conversation, they will say, "I was reading an *Official Game Critics* article where they said…." And in that context, it's pretty cool to be the default voice of *Official Game Critics*.

Previews

You can't have reviews without previews. Well, you could, but I don't know anybody who does. Previews are generally pretty easy to write, if only because you have limited data upon which to base your article. You might have a fact sheet, a press release, a handful of screenshots, an early build of one or two levels, or some mongrel combination. Take what you've got and do the best you can.

Whereas reviews are the final word on a game's quality, I feel previews should generally not be judgmental. Other people prefer to know the worst up front and want their previews to hit hard;

it's almost like they don't want to let themselves look forward to something later if there are any flaws now. But I maintain that the products are not complete and should not be held up to final standards yet. If you see things that are weak, certainly be honest and point them out, but it's really only fair to note that there is still time for these games to improve. Until that box is shrink-wrapped and on store shelves, anything can happen. (And it did once, in the case of a popular series of sports games. The preview version came in about six or seven weeks before release and it looked like the whole franchise was about to fumble. Then, miraculously, the last stretch of tweaking really did make all the difference, and the final product was totally polished. Never underestimate the power of talented programmers, a dedicated QA staff, and a lot of caffeine.)

The hard part about running the previews section is landing exclusives—first appearance of screens, first hands-on impressions, things like that. Most sites with exclusives post their stories a day or a weekend before everybody else, but they get a huge traffic and attention boost as a result. If you're not getting those scoops, all you can do is keep asking them, politely but regularly.

Features

Features are the true calling card of any publication. The reviews may be authoritative and the previews enlightening, but it's the features that give a media outlet its true personality and voice. This is both the most challenging and, understandably, the most rewarding section of most game publications. The creative freedom is high—there are no templates but the ones you choose to use—but the need for focus is, too, and not all writers are good at keeping focus for 2000 words.

What makes a good feature? A topic that's deep and rewarding enough that people will want to hold *their* focus for 2000 words.

You need a solid structure going in: The greatest games of all time, the role of women in the game industry, urban legends of gaming, how indie development is changing mass-market publishing, the business realities of a hardware shift…they've all been done, but you get the point. A good feature is generally one with a big focus, something that's been researched and is ready to be explained for your audience in satisfying detail.

Some features are just really long previews, but the trick is not making them fantastically boring. The game might be super cool and a huge scoop, but you still need to paint a larger picture in a feature article to justify the deluxe presentation. Interviews help a lot; sprinkling quotes from the developers always helps make a piece sound authoritative and wisely keeps the focus on the facts and the stars of the story. If, for instance, you get invited to see a new game at the developer's offices or studios, conveying your journey is effective too. Your readers will probably never get to walk down the halls of id Software or visit the Microsoft campus. Give them the chance to see what you see by using descriptive phrases and paint them a picture of your experience; approach it a little like travel journalism.

To a lesser extent, you can report on the people you interview in the same manner. Dropping in personal details of the interview itself can often be effective. What was your subject wearing? Did they smoke throughout the interview? Did you meet over lunch and find that they were vegetarian?

There is much more to writing a feature than just having a topic and coming up with an approach, but we'll leave it here for now because it could be a book on its own. The short version: A feature can be whatever you want it to be, but make sure you actually make it something specific.

Strategy

Online sites like GameFAQs.com offer timely, no-frills advice on even the most obscure games from writers who will tell you how to beat a game out of the sheer love of having beaten it themselves. However, some media sites also offer walkthroughs for action/adventure games, combo lists for fighters, locations of hidden items or shortcuts, targeted instructions on how to earn the toughest trophies and achievements, stuff like that. Sometimes it's easier to show than tell, so many sites specialize in video strategy guides or walkthroughs. It still needs to be written before it becomes a video, though.

Writing a strategy guide is a lot more work than you might expect. As a gamer, you know what questions you would ask about the game; when you sit down to tell other people those answers, you need to be very specific and clear. You will probably have to play the game several times—once to get through it, once to take notes, and once to get screenshots. It's very detail-oriented, and illustrative screens will only help you to a point. If you're the kind of person who likes explaining things in excruciating detail, you're perfect for strategy work. It drives some writers bonkers.

Letters

There are two ways to answer reader mail: Like a pal or like a jerk. Some readers write in questions to their favorite publications and expect a serious, friendly answer. Other readers love to see the editors rip on the idiots who ask dumb questions, and it's the only reason they read the letters section at all.

Honestly, there are compelling reasons for both approaches. The sarcasm is entertaining for the audience, but the earnest approach shows the readers that you're taking them seriously. If you answer one way, you will get letters asking you to do it the other way. Switch, and it's the same thing. It's information value versus entertainment value, and the audience is sharply divided on which they want, if not both at the same time.

Some outlets have found a way to do just that: Most letters in a weekly or monthly column are answered with a straight face, and in a small sidebar, they run a crazy letter or otherwise earmark a zone of the responses as less than serious. Whether or not you can get away with it depends greatly on your outlet's overall voice and attitude, but it doesn't hurt to get creative. For instance, I got tired of seeing the same questions appear over and over again in the mailbag—questions we'd already answered in previous issues—but I realized that the new readers asking were sincere and deserved answers. So I took all those "can I get a job at your magazine?" and "how come Nintendo doesn't release Mario games for the PlayStation?" questions and ran our responses in haiku. I stuck to the five-seven-five structure but still answered their questions with real facts and explanations. It was a fun creative challenge; I felt I had managed to both entertain the audience and respect their request for knowledge and insight. I would like to say that everybody else thought it was cool too, but after that letter column ran, not one reader wrote in with any reaction, good or bad. To this day, I don't know if the audience "got it." But if it was a failure, I think it was a noble one. I tried something different.

Community Management

Letters used to be the only way a reader could contact their favorite publication with feedback. Not any more—conversations bloom on Twitter, Facebook, and web forums, so someone from the media outlet needs to be part of that conversation. Some people see this role as a burden or an insult, but don't fool yourself: this kind of interaction is extremely important if you want to make sure you're really giving the reader what they want and expect.

Columns

In addition to the usual voices, many media outlets like to offer some editorial space to a guest in a column. That might be the same person every month, or it might be a soapbox occupied by a different orator every time. There's editorial value to both because readers check back to see what that person will say this time—or who that person will be. Someone on the editorial staff will need to reach out to those potential writers to develop and schedule those columns. It's worth it, as a little op-ed section can add a lot of personality.

Your publication may have all of those sections plus a few more; it may have none of the above. But how you run your section of the will largely be up to you, and no matter which one or ones you wind up overseeing, it's going to be a learning process the whole time.

Feature Attractions:
Heads, Decks, Sides, Subs, and More

In addition to all those words on the page, features generally incorporate three extra elements: a headline, a deck, and a subhead. They're easy for some people to create and a nightmare for others, but it's a skill worth acquiring.

The *headline* is what you'd think it would be—the title of the story. Sometimes they're designated as *hed* in a document, as that unnatural spelling sets it apart in a document so the layout artists know that it's a structural instruction, not article content. In newspapers, headlines are often very literal; "Dewey Defeats Truman" is a classic (if erroneous) example. In magazines and websites, however, you have the freedom to be more clever and creative. A non-literal headline can and should set the tone for the entire piece that follows it. For instance, when *GamePro* ran a feature story on *Gran Turismo 4*, the magazine could have gone with a simple, straightforward headline of "Gran Turismo Returns." But the article itself explained how *GT4* was going to be fundamentally different from the earlier games in the series. Combining that concept with a term from the world of auto racing resulted in "Sequential Shift." A sequential shifter is a style of gearshift used in racecars, but at the same time, this version of *GT* was a stylistic shift compared to the sequence of games that preceded it. It's not the greatest headline in the world, but it certainly played with the theme of the story a bit, it got the point across that there were changes in store for *Gran Turismo*, and it's arguably a lot more compelling than "Gran Turismo Returns." "Sequential Shift" implies something about the rest of the story and makes the reader who's just skimming stop and go "hmm." With a headline, you not only want to grab their attention, you want to take it a step further and make them wonder what that reference really means.

The *deck* (sometimes called a *strapline*, *slug*, or merely *dek* for the same reason stated above) tells readers a little more about what that headline means and what the story will be discussing, and it should do even more to pique the reader's curiosity. It shouldn't be long; two tight, short sentences is typically the perfect length because the deck is an informational tease, and the article itself is the payoff. If, in a case like the *GT4* story, your headline doesn't incorporate the name of the game itself, the deck must—don't rely on the art, the screenshots, or even the game logo to inform your audience about your topic. Step up and tell them. An old-school move is to end the deck with a question, such as, "But can it stay ahead with the competition gaining so fast?" Especially when you're talking about a popular franchise like *Gran Turismo*, this poses even more questions in the reader's mind, like, "Wait, what games are gaining? And what is *GT4*'s weakness that those other games might exploit?" If they want to know the answers, they will have to keep reading. It's an effective technique as long as it's not overused…and it can be overused fairly quickly. You should never see this twice in one issue, and if you can go a minimum of two issues between uses, that's even better.

A *subhead* (or just *sub*) is a mini-summary for the paragraphs that follow it; as the name implies, subheads are like the main headline, only on a smaller scale with more focus. Crucially, subheads help break up the body text so that it's not just one imposing brick of words that runs on for four pages. A subhead can also give the reader a place to pause, like a little landmark if they need to put down the article and return to it later, or a subhead can signal that the story is transitioning to another topic. In features about movie-related games, I've seen bits of dialogue lifted for use as the subheads (which is fine, as long as those bits of dialogue have relevance to the topics covered by the article). I've also seen quotes from the article's interview subjects be truncated and used as subheads. What you want to avoid are generic terms like "graphics" when introducing the segment about graphics—that's boring and uninviting. It gets the job done, but without style. Generally, the best unused puns and references generated in search of the head and deck later become subheads.

A *sidebar* (sometimes *side*) offers a related commentary or train of thought that doesn't necessarily fit in the main narrative, but is worth mentioning. You'll see these on longer reviews when the author wants to call special attention to some specific element of the game, such as flight mechanics or the quest system or the voice acting. They're also common for feature articles, so you should be ready to brainstorm and include them in any feature pitches.

Many publications like to use *pull quotes* to break up a layout. A pull quote is a short phrase or sentence from the article that serves a dual purpose: It's an art element to add variety to the layout, and it's an editorial statement to draw readers in. Pull quotes have to be able to exist as standalone statements, but they don't have to be summaries of the whole article; they're just teasers that would make someone want to say "What's the full story behind that?" These can be highly effective, and they don't take a lot of creative power to generate; you just have to look for them. For features or long reviews, be ready to nominate one or more lines as pull quotes for your editor.

Some publications use custom elements as well. *Official Xbox Magazine* features "bottom fillers" on every page—little factoids relevant to the article above, or a developer quote that came up during a demo, or maybe a personal anecdote about something funny that happened during the making of the article. These give *OXM* some extra personality, and they offer its writers a chance to be creative in a different way. If you write for a media outlet that does something along these lines, embrace the creative challenge.

REPRESENT!
Sooner or later, you'll wind up being the official embodiment of your media outlet. Here's how not to screw it up.

While the bulk of an editor's job is done behind a desk, inside a meeting room, or with a controller in hand, there are times when you will be called upon to leave the comfy confines of your cubicle and venture out into the real world. It's as scary as it sounds—and why would you want to leave this office after you worked so hard to get here?

Because the action is out there. E3 is a good example—the annual Electronic Entertainment Expo is the coming-out party for the entire industry, where new games are shown to the press and to retailers for the first time. It's loud, it's huge, and it's something you will need to cover, probably in real time. And when you're there, you'll wear a crucial badge with your name and publication on it, which identifies you as working media. Ta-da—you are now out in public as the guy from *Official Game Critics* who gave *Alien Shot* a low score.

Of course, there are smaller events than E3, where you could conceivably get lost in the madding crowds and never have to project your individual personality. There are pre-E3 media days, where publishers hold court in a big hotel or at their corporate headquarters and, with a captive audience of several dozen members of the press corps, show their big games before the show itself starts. The reason is kind of sad—E3 itself is too loud and too large and too hectic to get any real work done—but you've still got a name tag, still outing you as the guy from *Official Game Critics* who gave *Alien Shot* a low score.

On a more casual level, game publishers often throw "launch events" to celebrate the release of a game, at which time the press usually gets final reviewable code or boxed retail product, as well as some fancy finger food. You may or may not have a name tag at an event like this, and you may or may not want to hang out with the people you see in the room. But it's politically wise to attend if you're invited, and ultimately, it's yet another opportunity to be recognized as the guy from *Official Game Critics* who gave *Alien Shot* a low score.

Now, I hate to use the phrase "how to behave" to discuss the above situations because it sounds like something you tell toddlers who run around fancy restaurants as if they were playgrounds. However, as much as I hate it, it's accurate. I have seen many writers and editors embarrass themselves in similar ways. The job is fun, and sometimes the fun overtakes the professionalism, and that's when things get embarrassing for all involved. So, it's important to know how to...behave.

Whatever social skills you have, these public events are where they come into play. Just like any other job, a good part of being a game editor is working with people. You'll wind up meeting game developers, public relations staffers, producers, and of course, your peers in the press corps at E3, media days, and launch events. You're

watching all of them, but they're watching you, too. And, again, you
are the guy who did that article for that outlet last month. There's a
good chance that people in the room think they know you already.
You can either prove them right or prove them wrong by keeping a
few simple goals in mind.

Meet and greet

The PR staff will work the room, but chances are you'll find other
members of the press breaking off into groups. Despite what you
may think, game editors from different publications are not enemies,
and many do actually enjoy each others' company. It may be hard
at first, but don't be a social hermit; you're going to see these same
people over and over again at future events. It's not bad to recognize
someone's name and introduce yourself as a new person in the
industry, or say something nice about one of their articles. You gotta
make friends somehow, and if you just sit in the corner and nosh on
nachos, you'll be written off as the socially awkward newbie.

Stay sober

In the game industry, "launch event" is often synonymous with
"free booze." After two years in development, everybody associated
with the game is looking for closure, and a dog-and-pony show at a
trendy club with an open bar is the closure method of choice. And
when it's open bar, the folks mixing the drinks tend to be nice and
give you generous portions.

Obviously, you don't have to drink; nobody really needs to know
whether or not there's a little rum swirled in with your Coke. But
if you are going to drink at an industry event (and honestly, many
people around you will), know when to say when. Your primary
goal at these events should be not to embarrass yourself or your
publication, and when the hooch starts flowing, the risk goes up

exponentially. You do not want to be the guy in the industry whose name is immediately followed by, "Yeah, he got hammered at the *Alien Shot* event." They won't remember you for looking cool because you had a drink in your hand, but they will remember you for all the wrong reasons if you have too many drinks in your system.

Watch the gossip

Everybody has played a bad game, but a professional gathering is not the time to air grievances. It's only natural to want to get together with your friends and grouse about shared frustrations, but anybody could be listening to you and drawing conclusions. The publisher who might be considering signing a deal with the developer of the game you're slagging might think twice, or might think you're biased and ask that you not be invited next time. It would be easy for the developers within earshot to assume that they'll never get a fair shake from these media guys who have never programmed a game in their lives. Fellow press folks may enjoy the gossip, but they won't necessarily think that makes you employable down the road when they have a position to fill. Plus, the PR person will wonder what terrible things you say about *their* games when you are at other companies' events. And just to make you ultra-paranoid, some people use these situations as a chance to *gather* info, hoping that your loose lips will help them sink ships. One editor I know used to go to events largely for recon, to find out what the competition was up to, and he would always report back. Do you really want to help him?

It's okay to discuss work with peers and colleagues, but just as you should avoid taking the cheap shots in your articles, avoid taking cheap shots in person, too. They can come back to hurt you later.

Don't forget to do some work

Some launch events are pure parties, complete with loud DJ and epileptic lighting. Others are actually intended to impart information or might be your only chance to speak face to face with the developer. Look for the monitor where the game being celebrated is actually running, and go over to get a demo. Even if you already know what you need to know about the game (or think you know what you need to know), someone was flown to that event for the express purpose of demonstrating the game to the press. Be open-minded and let them do their job. Ask a few intelligent questions, take notes where applicable and pick up the controller when it's offered to you. Offer your business card at the end and thank them. That game demo is why you're there.

Some outlets may have policies about how long you can stay and what you're allowed to do at an event. After all, if you're getting too chummy, it might cloud your judgment, or lead to the perception that you are no longer impartial. Doesn't matter if that perception is true; the damage is done. So check with your editor before you check your coat.

Bottom line, even though a lot of these events have a social feel to them, you must remember that you are still on the clock and that you are still working for your publication merely by attending. What you do, what you say, and how you...behave...matter to everyone in attendance, as well as some who aren't.

Dress for Success

Two words game editors never want to hear is "dress code." One of the luxuries of the job is that every day is Casual Friday. But when you're representing the publication at an industry event or, worse, on TV, some common-sense guidelines will save you some trouble.

Don't wear Company A's t-shirt to Company B's event

This is a bit insensitive. You're being given a sales pitch on Company B's products; respect them enough to at least let them do their thing without being a distraction. Company B knows you play Company A's games; it's just tacky to give Company A free advertising at Company B's party.

Don't wear Company A's t-shirt to Company A's event.

This is no better. It just makes you look like a kiss-ass.

Don't wear anybody's t-shirt if you're hosting an event

If your own editorial outlet is sponsoring the shindig, go business casual. Wear something with buttons, like a simple oxford or a golf shirt. This should be a logo-free shirt, which is different from a shirt with a logo that you got for free.

    The one exception to any of the above: I am a big fan of wearing my *own* company's shirt. Self-promotion never goes out of style. I always try to do this for TV appearances and generally wear my own brand's logo if I'm going to visit a developer—not only to reinforce my outlet is one so interested in their work that they want to come see it in person, but also as a kind warning that there is a *spy in the house*! The developers know who the marked man is at all times, and if there's something they can't show me yet, they know to put it away before I get too close. Other people think it's cheesy, but I see it as a little courtesy, paid forward.

PROS AT CONS

A few times a year, the videogame industry gathers to learn, show off, and/or party at public and trade events. What are you doing here?

Sooner or later, if you have scored a staff position at a publication, freelanced enough work, and/or have a part-time job at a game retailer, you will find yourself on assignment at a trade show or gaming convention—Tokyo Game Show, the Game Developer's Conference, Penny Arcade Expo, San Diego Comic-Con, or any one of a number of other events. There are meetings, there are parties, there are interviews, there are freebies. It's probably very loud. It's very large. It's very tiring. And yes, it's fun. But as a working journalist, you will have responsibilities that must come first. Trade shows are tough to cover; you can't be everywhere at once, and whatever you see or do will probably have to be written up immediately. Before you step into that convention center, wherever it may be located, be prepared for work.

Make a week of it

A trade show might last longer than advertised. While E3 itself might officially start on a Wednesday, the pre-E3 events take place the two days before. Sony, Microsoft, and Nintendo usually host press conferences during that time. Before booking your flight and hotel, find out what crucial pre-events are going down, and schedule your trip for more than just the show itself.

Dress appropriately

All that stuff in the Dress for Success section applies here. Wear neutral, business-casual clothing, unless your publication has other rules. Some folks like to attend shows in full three-piece suits; if that makes you feel confident and professional, go for it. There's no shame in getting dressed up for the big dance, but there is shame in looking like a slob.

Wear comfortable shoes

You will often walk several miles a day during a trade show. Every year before E3, I get new insoles, if not new shoes. If the Shoe Edict conflicts with the Dress for Success edict, go shopping. Get some simple, unadorned black sneakers made for intense walking.

Make appointments—and keep them

The best way to see the biggest games at any trade show—and the best way to make strong contacts with publishers—is to make a personal appointments. Publishers' time is valuable, and they don't make an appointment unless they expect you to show. Besides, you will want this opportunity to ask questions about the products, meet people in person who you've only spoken to on the phone and in email, and swap business cards.

Schedule wisely

Most appointments last between a half an hour and an hour, so even if you book a meeting for every half hour (and can somehow get to all those places in time), you won't be able to see everybody and everything at the show. You'll need to prioritize what you want to see and what you have to see. One appointment an hour really gives you enough time to talk and learn, but some publishers simply can't spare that much time. This is also why many publishers now have elaborate "editor's days," because the trade shows are simply too hectic and too time-compressed to get enough done.

You'll also want to plan your schedule based on the lay of the land. Get the map of the convention center or city where the convention will take place and plan your appointments with the layout in mind. Getting from meeting A to meeting B and arriving at all your appointments on time is not easy. The first time I went to E3, I made the mistake of making appointments every half-hour. I wanted to meet everybody! Unfortunately I had no prior knowledge of the layout of the Los Angeles Convention Center and found myself running at top speed between the West and South Halls, sweating like a pig. I have some embarrassing photos from that show that I will not reproduce here.

Take notes during every meeting

You might get a press kit, but you also want to be ready to write down your own thoughts. I used to take notes with a paper and pen, and many still do, but I've found bringing a laptop or tablet with a wireless keyboard to be worth the weight. I type much faster than I write longhand, so I can get more info and direct quotes down as they happen. And even then, I keep a pad of paper and several pens with me just in case. Do whatever works for you, because you can't write online news reports without raw data.

Drink responsibly

For some people, game trade shows are about games. For others, it's the parties at night. A prime reason for people not keeping their appointments is that they went to a sponsored party the night before and they're too hung over to work the show the next day. If you came into the office too hung over to work, you'd be in huge trouble, but somehow it's okay on the road? Nope. Show up ready to do your job, not ready to fall asleep in a puddle of your own vomit.

Greed is bad

If a PR rep or booth attendant wants to give you a t-shirt, and you feel comfortable accepting it, that's cool. But to stalk the show, scamming for the best booth and ask "What do you have for free?" That's crass and inappropriate. But you will see people do it. If the acquisition of freebies is why you're at the show, you should not be at the show.

Bring cash and save your receipts

Whether you're going to be reimbursed by your company or you wind up footing the bill as an independent freelancer, you will be amazed at how quickly you go through money at an event. Plane fare is a few hundred bucks; a hotel stay will probably cost a bit more. Cabs and shuttles are often the main way to get around from the airport to your hotel to the show and to the evening events, and they cost money too. Food at the convention center is overpriced and less than satisfying, too. Hit the ATM and try to keep yourself on a budget, but keep an eye on it all. And save those receipts, so you can either be reimbursed.

GOING ON THE RECORD

Sometimes you're the interviewer, sometimes you're the interviewee. Here's your heads-up guide to talking heads.

One of your editorial duties is to get the info on upcoming releases. How do you learn what's coming if you don't ask? You'll need to get on the phone to the game publisher's PR department and start asking questions. That's a form of interviewing.

The word "interview" usually makes people think of a straight-up, one-to-one conversation with some notable figure in the industry for a verbatim Q&A session. Maybe you're interviewing a person to get their comments in relation to another story you're working on, such as a developer or retailer's view on how piracy affects their business. Those are both forms of interviewing, but they're not the only ones, nor is either the type that you'll wind up using most frequently.

Companies will come to your office and show you a private

demo of a game with the producer and/or developer in tow. This is fairly common; two or three press tours happen on any given week, more during the busy pre-holiday season in the fall. And although you are not wearing a name tag, you will be handing over your business card, which identifies you as the guy from *Official Game Critics* who gave *Alien Shot* a low score. Naturally, you just handed your card to the *Alien Shot* developer.

These demos, whether conducted in your office, their office, or on neutral ground, such as a hotel suite, are essentially interviews. It's you, talking to someone who knows more than you do, who is willing to give you information. All you have to do is ask the right questions.

In all cases, you need to be prepared to get the information you need, politely and professionally.

Do your homework

Conduct some research before you go into a game demo. Know something about the title if you can; if not, at least familiarize yourself with the publisher and, if you know it before the demo itself, the developer. If the nature of your interview is more of a personality profile, then obviously a lot more preparation has to go into it, but just knowing the last game the developer created can help you put the information you're about to receive into context. What's more, it shows respect for the people in the room if you can speak intelligently about their work; don't insult them or waste their time by not being prepared to talk to them specifically.

Questions, please

Writing questions ahead of time (or at least bringing a list of discussion topics with you) is a smart idea. Of course, it will be boring if you just read them verbatim, but better to do that and make sure you ask the right questions in the right way than try to wing it and trip over your tongue. On the same note, you should be paying attention to what the interviewee says and sculpt your follow-up questions to match. It's not uncommon to walk into a demo with a list of a dozen questions only to have the developer answer the first nine as part of their standard intro, so keep track of what they've already said. The more like a natural conversation your interview sounds, the better the responses will be, and the stronger the resulting article.

The best questions are the ones without easy answers. Always ask open-ended questions like "what are you hoping to add to the genre with this game?" and "what did the previous game teach you that you were able to implement here?" rather than just-the-facts queries like "this has been in development for nine months, right?" If a question can be answered with a simple "yes" or "no" or "actually, ten," the respondent has nowhere to go. Create questions that force your subject to come up with the answer in their own words. Their personality will shine through in the resulting story, and you'll get far more useful data this way.

Play nice with others

Sometimes, your interview will not be one-on-one; it'll be eight-on-one as the dev team tries to handle questions from eight different media outlets simultaneously. This might be due to time constraints, or it might be simply because the team doesn't want to run eight gauntlets. Be ready to lead or follow in these situations, and respect the flow of the conversation—but make sure you ask your most important questions before the timer goes off. If you don't, let the PR person know that you'd like to get a few things answered before you leave or set up a phone interview for later.

Respect "off the record"

This comes down to personal integrity and honor. If someone says something that is *off the record*, that means it's just for your personal background knowledge and not for publication. Most often it's when a developer brings up a feature that they'd like to include in the game but it hasn't been finalized and might not make it in, so they don't want to officially say it in the interview, get everybody's hopes up, and then have to cut it because they were never sure in the first place. On rare occasions, it's something juicier. But whatever it may be, if it's off the record, keep it to yourself.

Deep background is another term sometimes used for information not to be included in the article, but discussed for a better understanding of the subject matter. Off-the-record information is info that can be sourced to your interviewee; deep background is stuff that might come up, but the source is someone other than your interviewee, and as such, needs to be fact-checked independently by you if you find it useful.

Record it

Direct quotes from your interview subject can add a lot of power to your article, and having a recording device is crucial for getting quotes down correctly. I use a small digital audio recorder and download the files for transcription later. For phone interviews, you will want a device that lets you tap into a telephone line and route the audio to a recorder, so you can record both sides of the call. They sell this kind of doohickey at Radio Shack. Alternatively you can use recording software with voice-over-IP chat programs; I have had good luck with Pamela, a third-party recording plug-in for Skype.

It's also crucial that you get permission to record. Every state has its own law about recording conversations, so check your state's rules (they're easily found online). In some cases, it's legally required to get explicit permission from both parties before recording. Ethically, it's appropriate (and just plain courteous) to ask before pressing Record, though most people understand that they are meeting you with the express purpose of having what they say be used in an article. I don't think I've ever had anybody object to my recording their interview, but it is professional and polite—not to mention legal—to ask before you begin.

Take notes

A tape recorder is no excuse for not scribbling madly during a demo or interview. Recorders break, batteries die, tapes run out, and background noise can render even the most advanced recording device totally worthless. You should take notes throughout your session in addition to whatever you think you're recording. Again, I recommend a laptop or humble pen and paper as the ultimate backup.

Wake up

Yawning in a game demo is bad. It may be involuntary, it may have absolutely nothing to do with the quality of the game you are looking at, but it's still a horrible message to send to the developer who got on a plane to show his baby to the world for the first time. I am a serial yawner in demos, because I often keep late hours and then go in the next day really tired. By the time a 2pm demo comes in, I'm ready for a nap. Plan ahead, get to bed at a reasonable time the night before a company is coming in, and be ready to actually do your job the next day. If that fails, chug an energy drink half an hour before the meeting.

Once the interview is done, the work begins. Transcribing the interview is a pain in the ass. It will likely take you four times longer to transcribe than it did to record; if your conversation lasted a half-hour, you'll be spending two full hours just typing in what was said. I did a two-hour interview with a major game developer that resulted in a mammoth, eight-hour transcription session, but it was worth it—it turned into a large print feature and two online articles.

These basics of interviewing are also the basics of actual journalism. This is what it takes to go out and get the story, and it's just another facet to being a full-time game editor.

Quote, Edit, Unquote?

Running any sort of direct quote becomes an ethical quandary because you have to define the nature of "direct quote." If your interviewee stumbled over their words or changed direction in the middle of a sentence (which we all do in natural conversation, but rarely realize until we hear ourselves played back), do you print exactly what was said, down to the individual stammers, or do you fix it so they sound intelligent and coherent, even if that's not actually what they said? If the subject makes a grammatical error, do you go with what you know they meant and "fix" the quote?

Case in point: One year at E3, as he was discussing the PlayStation 2's market dominance, Sony Computer Entertainment president Kaz Hirai announced to a crowd of journalists, "The console wars is over." Everybody knew he meant "are" instead of "is." I didn't feel it was necessary to make him look bad, so in the resulting news story, I changed it to "are." However, because so many other reporters were in attendance, many other outlets printed his gaffe as it was said. Was it out of a sense of journalistic accuracy, or were they taking unfair advantage of a prominent and powerful man making a mistake? As it was, I caught heat from friends at other publications for fixing the quote; they said I should have left it as he said it. I still think I did the right thing.

There was another time that I did a phone interview with a game sound designer for a high-profile story in a major magazine. Unfortunately, there was a hiccup on the recording and a word was missing in the middle of a really good comment. His work has a sense of whimsy to it, so in the process of reconstructing the phrase, I replaced the missing adjective with the word "wacky" without consulting him. The story ran that way, and while he liked the piece (and was grateful for the attention and new business it brought him), he was disappointed to see that word in there, because it's simply not something he even would have said; it was not a way he would have described himself or his work. He wished I'd just called him to pick a new, mutually agreeable word. I should have. It was a bad edit on my part, and it's something I still regret. I took it as a life lesson.

So it's tricky. There are some who feel that if it's said, it's law— you as the reporter do not have the right to alter someone else's words. But I am much more lenient in this regard, and I think of how it will look to the reader. I never want to change the meaning of a quote, but if someone's phrasing prevents that meaning from being understood, I will tweak it for clarity. I don't want to embarrass the subject by making them sound stupid, and I don't want the reader to be confused by what was said. This does *not* grant me license to change things wholesale the way I did with the sound designer, but as an editor, I value the flow, readability, and comprehension of a story over the nitpicky precision of a transcription.

Media Interviewing Media

Interviewing someone for a story is one thing; being interviewed as a representative of the gaming media for someone else's story is totally different. Whether it's for a newspaper story, a radio program, or a TV spot, you're in the hot seat to come up with clever, concise answers for someone else's questions. When you are the interview subject, you suddenly gain an appreciation for what you put everybody else through.

Not everybody will be called on to go on G4TV and talk about the best games of the year, but if you are, there are some things to keep in mind:

Do your homework

This again? Yep. Find out the topic ahead of time, consider the potential audience for the story (are you being interviewed by the *New York Times* or *Boys Life*?), look up some useful bits of info to support your thoughts on the subject, and have your story straight. The media outlet called you as an expert to lend flavor to *their* story, so you know better than anybody what kind of information they will find most useful. Be ready to give it to them.

Know how to pronounce game names and characters before going on TV

This can be really embarrassing, especially if some of the names are Japanese and you're not. If need be, call the company's PR team and ask them for the proper pronunciation.

If you're talking about a specific game, know how to play it

I was flattered to be asked to be interviewed for a cable TV program the day after Christmas, and the show said they wanted me to play some games live on the air and demonstrate some strategy tips to people who might have just received them as holiday gifts the day before. Unfortunately, the games they wanted to show were the ones with which I had no experience, let alone aptitude, but the magazine didn't want to turn down the opportunity for some killer exposure. So I crammed for three days before the show, trying to get these games down so I could seem competent on the air, and ultimately failed. As it was, the show didn't have time to have me play live; they just had me talk to the host while stock footage of gameplay rolled. Just as well, because I felt pretty unprepared. Don't let the desire to get your mug on TV (or the magazine's desire for free advertising) overshadow the fact that you simply might not be the right person to do it.

Clean up your act
Shave. Comb. Scrub. Whatever. You're about to be beamed into millions of homes. You don't have to act like a star, but you should at least shower like one. This goes for wearing presentable clothing, too.

Watch your mouth
Hey, we all make mistakes, but remember: This is the ultimate form of representing your employer. You do not want to be the star of one of those funny YouTube clips that people pass around where the guy being interviewed used foul language and embarrassed himself and the network. You have just as much chance of making a good impression as making a career-ending one.

ACCOUNTABILITY II: THE EDITING

It's not just what you let the writers write.
Well, actually, it is.

Remember MonkeyGamer7598? He's the guy who thought he'd turn his love of Internet insults into a career, and now he's writing game reviews, possibly aided and abetted by this very book. Let's assume he has ignored most of the book's advice and skipped the part about accountability altogether because he wanted to know how to contact you, the editor at his favorite publication. Now take it a step further: MonkeyGamer7598 is your brand-new intern, learning the ropes, and you assigned him his first bylined article. And when his unaccountable, indefensible, irresponsible copy arrives on your desk, it's suddenly your problem to solve.

As it was when you were a freelance writer, being accountable for what your publication prints is crucial as an editor; it's part of your basic responsibilities. If you write a review and say a game is bad, you already know you have to explain why. But your publication will be blamed for anything you can't, in good conscience, explain or defend, whether you personally wrote it or not...and readers hold grudges. If they're really angry, they remember your name and approach each of your future articles with a bias—"That's the guy who gave *Alien Shot* a low score and said he'd rather drink a cup of someone else's urine than have to play it again." If you need to adjust a review score or rewrite some of the copy in order to make an article defensible, now's the time, because once it's out there, you're responsible for it.

Furthermore, you're not just accountable to the readers; you're accountable, in part, to the game publishers. Without caving in to pressure or being accused of rampant fanboyism (or worse, corruption), you obviously want to keep your relationship with the game companies strong. If they think you're printing low reviews for reasons other than software quality, or if your articles don't actually support your scores, you will hear about it. Unfortunately, you'll probably hear about it through your publisher, CEO, or some other terrifying form of your boss's boss, because when game companies get angry, they don't screw around—they go right to the top, and then it trickles down the entire chain of command to you. And like readers, companies hold grudges, too. There are some publishers who simply refuse to work with certain writers or publications who they feel have wronged them or are not taking responsibility for what they write. You need them, but they don't really need you.

Of course, there's the other side of the equation to consider. Once you start remixing the freelancer's copy, egos get bruised, and people get hurt. But anything that you feel is really, really off-base in its judgment calls for a rewrite, which is one of the many weapons in the editor's arsenal. Do not just change it to be what you want it to be and run it without discussing it with the writer; call them, tell them what doesn't work for you, and discuss it to find a middle ground or, at the very least, help them understand why what they submitted ain't ready for the big time. If you have to reassign a review because you think the first writer was off his rocker, so be it—pay the first person a kill fee and think twice about hiring them next time. But let that writer know what's going on and that you are changing the plan for the good of the mag or site.

As an editor, it's easy to put yourself in the writer's position. You want to let them keep the sense of voice and personal expression that you yourself value and enjoy. Nobody *likes* being edited. Everybody likes to think they don't need correction. But ultimately, the final score that a publication levies is the magazine's call. Some publications have regular meetings to discuss the merits of the scores, and they adjust them as a staff based on what the outlet has stated in the past about that genre or franchise and what each of them thought when they played it. The freelancers are not running the show, and they are not going to get in the same amount of trouble you will if something goes out that's simply wrong. You have the power, and in this case, you have to wield it for the good of everyone involved.

THE INEVITABLE CRY OF BIAS!

It's a word that you should understand, even if your readers don't

"Official Game Critics gave *Alien Shot* a 9? I knew they would! They're so obviously biased!"

When I see the word "biased," the hairs on the back of my neck go up. I think people use the word far too quickly without understanding what they're saying. With the freedom to say whatever the heck you want in an Internet discussion, it's an easy cheap shot that can and will be taken at the slightest disagreement. And the days of writing a strongly worded letter to the editor are gone; through social media, the readers can and will insinuate about, question, and insult you directly, whether they have a legitimate claim or not.

Semantic time again. The Free Online Dictionary defines bias as "a preference or an inclination, especially one that inhibits impartial judgment." The only bias I've seen in most reviews is that writers tend to give the games they like high scores, and the games they don't like get low scores. Strangely, they prefer games that they enjoyed playing. As has been stated previously, a review *must* be an opinion. It should be an opinion that is formed impartially, based on the experience of playing the game (and a few others) and nothing else. I think the bulk of the people who write reviews professionally understand this (or else they'd be out of a job very fast). If that's not the case—if there's something else influencing that decision beyond what happens between playing the game and writing the review— then there might be a legitimate accusation of bias.

Alleging bias is like taking credit for inventing a pop culture catchphrase: It's easy to claim but hard to prove. If you want to truly accuse someone of bias, you'll need a lot of data to make that case, things like several examples of high scores for one company in particular that go against the bulk of the other scores, for instance, or examples of empty praise that isn't backed up with the text of the review. Most people who shout "bias!" in a crowded web forum honestly cannot point to examples to prove their allegation. But that will not stop them from shouting "bias!" at you, even if they can't (or won't, or never intend to) prove it. The damage is done.

The solution, for when this inevitably happens to something your outlet has published, is to explain it this way: A reader disagreeing with your review does not make you biased. It just means you have different opinions. Your opinion was backed up with X number of words; upon what are they basing their allegation of bias? Their response should be at least that many words, and twice as compelling. It may not end cleanly and calmly, but you will have taken a logical stand and shown the readers that, yes, you're out there, and yes, you can hear them when they express an opinion.

And good luck fighting people on the Internet. You're on your own there.

READERS AND HOW TO TAME THEM

We have met the audience, and they are us. Now it's time to talk to yourself

Now that you've clawed your way to respectability and you are getting paid to play videogames for a living, don't forget about the little people—namely, your audience. Staying in touch with the readers is hugely undervalued and reader goodwill is an alarmingly powerful thing. I really feel strongly that it should be one of the basic responsibilities of being a full-time editor.

Treat reader questions with respect

If you want to give sarcastic answers for humorous effect in the letters column, that's fine—just don't do it on *every* letter. A lot of people who take the time to write in are doing so because they genuinely want a straight answer about a topic that they care about from someone they consider an expert or an authoritative source. Give them the basic respect of a decent answer. You cannot answer every letter personally, though sometimes it's worth it, depending on the question and your schedule.

Post in your publication's online forums

This also goes for your Facebook and Twitter outposts, or any other community portal your outlet chooses to create. Even if you stick your nose in for 15 minutes every other day, your presence does some good. When readers see that the editors are regularly involved in the community areas, it lets them know that you care that they have chosen to spend their leisure time in your digital space. Even if the last thing you would like to do on any given day is get into an online flame war with a kid who is amazingly jealous of your job, sometimes it's worth it. How you react will either convert that person (yes, it has happened) or convert everybody who's reading the exchange—your pub's respect quotient can go way up if you act with a bit of maturity and take the core of the complaint to heart. Show a sense of humor, post in the topics they create, comment on their ideas for your publication. Be a human being. You may be amazed at the results.

Explain things

Sometimes readers will ask questions about the process of making your publication—like "how did you get this game so early" and "why do you keep redesigning the home page with ads that take up all the extra space"—and sometimes those questions are going to be asked in a rude manner. Tackle them anyway. The simple truth is that very often these basic process questions go unanswered because nobody wants to take the time to explain them. Maybe it's a FAQ in the forums, maybe it's a form letter that you have saved to your hard drive that you send out to individuals. But this is the equivalent of a directory's commentary track on a DVD: Only you know the secrets of how this magical thing came to life. Within reason, there's no harm in revealing them if someone's really curious. If you give them insight, they will often give you loyalty.

Take your lumps

For some reason, many readers expect you never, ever, ever to make a mistake, but goofs are inevitable. When you do goof, admit it. Whether or not you apologize is up to you, but again, even just acknowledging that there was a miscommunication or an error gives you credibility as a publication and a person. Every time I've seen a media outlet try to wiggle out or create a lie around a mistake, the readers see right through it and hold it against them for a long, long time. Ask yourself: Is whatever went wrong really so bad that you have to lie to the people who make your publication successful? Deal with it like an adult and move on.

The people who read your publication are who you used to be— hopefully, who you still are when you're not wearing your company hat. They are out there, and they want some acknowledgement. It doesn't take long, it's not difficult, and it can pay off in massive loyalty dividends down the road.

Are You Already Obsolete?

Here's a terrifying thought: When every gamer is armed with a keyboard and a smart mouth, does anybody really care what critics say? Did you spend all this time honing your chops just to be replaced by a Twitter search?

When he was writing for *Newsweek*, game journalist N'Gai Croal suggested that traditional game critique is already dead and doesn't know it. Game fans are savvy, smart, sarcastic, and more than eager to share their opinions through web forums or blogs. If the peer group of gamers is mobilized and discussing what's good and bad in gaming as a community, don't their standards trump some professional blowhard who thinks his opinion is better than everybody else's?

Well, while I do see the logic there, I also know what they say about opinions—everyone's got them, just like certain parts of the anatomy. But everyone doesn't have a *qualified* opinion. Someone who spends all their time considering the ins and outs of the games they play, someone who has created or at least tried to create games themselves, someone who truly *studies* the history, development, and social aspects of games is, at least in theory, more qualified to pass judgment than some blogging blowhard who thinks his opinion is better than everybody else's.

I think critique is only as valuable as the critics themselves make it. I say it often because I truly believe it: You're only as good as your last review. If you want to be trusted as a source of information, you'll have to earn it with every article. A lazy critic is a critic who doesn't deserve to be turned to as an expert source anyway. And just like you don't always trust your friends' tastes, you won't always trust a critic's tastes to match up with your own—that's only natural. But that doesn't mean either set of opinions is totally worthless or that those disagreements won't help you make up your own mind.

Ultimately, it's true that it is up to the audience to decide what they find valuable. And maybe one day, the audience will decide that critics hold no value, and we will be extinct altogether. But I don't see that happening soon. For one, criticism has to evolve to remain useful to the audience, so right there, you're assuming that criticism can't change with the times—silly, if you look at the history of criticism in other media. Being aware of the audience's needs and serving them is what will keep critique from dying out.

In other words, don't slack, or you're dead. But you're not dead until you slack.

"HOW MUCH IS YOUR OPINION?"

Do advertisers buy favorable reviews? Are you really just a pawn in some advertising scam?

"How much do you charge a company to give their game a good review?"

Oh, here we go. Just the phrasing suggests that you're already dealing with someone who's made up their mind. "You're corrupt, right?"

There's a separation between the editorial and advertising departments at an outlet for a reason. And yet, the publisher straddles the line between the business and creative worlds. The truth is that, depending on their personal moral fiber, they can and will influence editorial decisions. That can be as subtle and helpful as analyzing the numbers and noting which subjects have performed particularly well, or it can be as slimy and direct as going out to lunch with a game publisher and coming back with a mandatory suggestion to put one of that publisher's games on the cover of the next issue or a nice week-long special website event. Is their suggestion for coverage coming from a strategic study of the market, or is it coming from a desire to secure ads from an influential business partner?

The problem is that the website's top story or magazine's cover feature is an editorial creation, but the real estate it occupies is often seen as more of a sales tool. When a game appears on a magazine cover or on the front page of a website, it clearly benefits both the publication and the game's publisher. It's a big, juicy billboard for two products at once. Having the most attractive image of the hottest game associated with your publication can make a difference, both in fiscal matters and in public perception. The fiscal stuff is truly the responsibility of the ad sales staff, so their influence over the look of the product they're trying to sell makes a certain amount of sense. It's a biz thing.

So maybe the real problem is the big feature that matches that front page. The ad guys aren't responsible for what goes in that editorial space; if the editor-in-chief feels there's a better story out there that's of more interest to the readers, they might fight for that, or they might still trust the ad team's advice over their own intuition. Ask any monarch with a council of advisors. The choice between your own instincts and the instincts of your team is a hell of a difficult decision to make. Even though it happens often, it never gets any easier.

Really, unless you're the EiC, the cover subject is something that you don't get to influence. You're not the publisher. You're an editor; you play the games and write about them, and you can chime in if and when you're asked. But you'll be blamed for whatever ethical lapses the money hats succumb to, and even a few that they don't, simply because sometimes the audience will assume the worst.

The audience certainly assumed the worst in late 2007, when

GameSpot editor Jeff Gerstmann was unceremoniously fired after working there for a decade. The whole mess centered around a middling review for Eidos' *Kane & Lynch: Dead Men* that appeared at the same time that Eidos had bought major ad space on the site. The peanut gallery put two and two together and assumed he was let go for biting the advertising hand that feeds. GameSpot and Eidos denied it, but neither party would comment on the real reason (and legally, Jeff can't discuss it). It was handled poorly, and assumptions were given credence simply because there was no timely response to dispel them. Meanwhile, some readers therefore assumed all media outlets were as corrupt as they'd always hoped they might be ("No *wonder* they didn't agree with me on *Alien Shot II*! They're all on the take!") and called for boycotts of both GameSpot and Eidos. There was a lot of drama.

Was it true? Was there more to the story? Who knows. "GerstmannGate" ultimately called the ethics of the entire gaming press into question, even if the actual "evidence" was circumstantial and everybody involved was operating under gag orders. Not the proudest day for game-journalism ethics, but maybe, ultimately, an important step. Who would even consider trying to buy an opinion after that?

I don't want to believe the worst, but I'm not naïve either. I suspect it has happened, moreso in the old days than now. And at places I've worked, I've seen influence crop up as subtly as "strong suggestions" and as bold as simple instructions like "this is your big story for December." Sometimes that's been the same A-list title that the edit staff felt was the best choice anyway, and sometimes not. The only real ethical question is where those cover suggestions come from and why, and whether the editorial staff follows them or not. Like many ethical issues, it comes down to trusting individuals.

So...how much does an opinion cost? I don't really know

because I've never sold one. As an editor, you can only work for what you believe is the right story, and then trust that at your publication's content isn't really for sale in the first place.

Write What You Think, Not What You Hear

Sometimes, a game publisher will try to exert an influence over you directly. Most PR people understand that they can encourage a position but not dictate what you write, but there are exceptions to every rule. And a publisher's influence can be very subtle—so subtle, you might not even realize you're being influenced.

A few years back, a major game from a major publisher came with a major push from the PR team. The demos for that game were loosely scripted but strongly focused, which is pretty standard; specific phrases were used in the presentation to convey the core points that they wanted the press to know.

The problem: Those same exact turns of phrase appeared in the resulting reviews. The game scored very high across the board, but much of the glowing praise used the same phrases that we all heard in our identical product demos and presentations. Had the publisher managed to cunningly dictate the thoughts of a large chunk of the press? Once you see a pattern emerge, it's hard not to doubt the validity of those reviews with the matching high scores. Did they really think it was great…or did they *think* they thought it was great?

PR presentations are full of useful information; they tell you what the publisher intends with and thinks about its own game, which is a good angle to consider in your coverage. But those presentations are also rehearsed, and you must be careful to not become a part of their performance.

LEVEL 4 KEEPING IT

■LEVEL 5■

Saving It

The road to success is fraught with danger. You'll face ethical quandaries, difficult personal issues, and you might even get to the point where you want to stop doing this thing altogether. Here's how to handle the darkest days of your career.

FREEBIES, TCHOTCHKES, AND "PLAYOLA"
What's the price of your opinion?
It's probably not as low as everybody thinks

The videogame industry is largely about promotion. Games that get a lot of attention generally wind up selling better. If a game appears on the cover of a magazine, it sits on the newsstand for a month and everybody who sees it, whether or not they buy it, gets the impression of that game. Same goes for editorial events on websites ("It's *Alien Shot* week here at *Official Game Critics!*"), with new screens and developer interviews and whatnot each day of that week. Whether or not you consider covers and front-page events to be "free ads," it's certainly a promotional tool for both the game's publisher and the editorial outlet. They're both hoping that you pick up the issue or click through to the features based on that featured image.

But, naturally, with only so many magazine covers and website homepages in a given month, real estate is scarce. Everybody wants their game to get more attention, often by any means necessary.

Billboards and TV advertising only go so far; a lot of games are sold by word of mouth. Friends tell friends about a cool game coming out, or a game they can play together online. The newbie gets converted. And where did the pro get their information—how did they know it was going to be a cool game? They probably read something about it.

So. Getting your game media attention becomes a pretty big deal. And with hundreds of games shipping annually, how do you get your game to stand out to the press corps that is drowning in information about everybody else's games? Generally with press tours, live demos, and the inevitable tchotchkes.

Tchotchkes (pronounced "chotch-keys") is the Yiddish word for "trinkets," and the computer and tech industry uses the term alongside the more common "swag." Baseball caps, letter openers, small toys, t-shirts—all emblazoned with a logo or a character, a physical reminder of someone's important game that they can leave behind for the editors to keep, use, play with, or pass on to the readers as contest prizes. They give it to you so you'll put it on your desk or wear it to the mall and remind yourself or others that this is an important game worthy of a baseball cap, letter opener, small toy, or t-shirt. Sometimes they're quite clever, such as the single combat boot that was sent out with instructions to go buy a melon, draw a face on it, and practice stomping zombie heads in preparation for *Resident Evil*. Clever or not, they're all promotional. They're all tchotchkes.

Chris Kramer, who's handled PR campaigns for Sony Online, Capcom, and many other publishers, says, "A lot of times when I design a tchotchke, it's something that goes on a desk, a body, or a vehicle and displays something about that game that will keep it directly or subliminally top-of-mind. If I send you a really nice sword with the *EverQuest II* logo lasered into it, and '5 of 200' lasered into the back, and a rack, I have done everything but come to your office and screw that into the wall. You're gonna go, 'Man, this is awesome,' and you're going to put that sword up. And people are going to come into your office and say, 'Wow, you have an *EverQuest II* sword—where did that come from?' And you're gonna say, 'From the *EverQuest II* people!' And in that conversation, you just said *EverQuest II* two or three times."

Matt Schlosberg, who worked in PR on behalf of companies like Acclaim and 2K Games, agrees that the primary goal is to keep a game's awareness high, but there's another benefit to a well-executed tchotchke: "It shows that we as a company are really getting behind it. This isn't just some budget title that we're throwing out the door and hoping it's a success; this is a game that warrants extra dollars, time, and energy to ensure that people know about it and want to learn more."

Matt adds that this, in fact, works, like when he mailed out chocolate bars during American Chocolate Week (March 14-20—exactly one week after Dentist's Day!) to promote the then-embargoed *Charlie and the Chocolate Factory* videogame, based on the Tim Burton film. "My hands were pretty tied with the information and assets I was allowed to release, because it was a big licensed title and we were not allowed to get ahead of the PR for film. So, by sending out the chocolate, it piqued people's interest, and we received requests to cover the game."

Innocent, right? It was American Chocolate Week, for cryin' out loud. But sometimes, tchotchkes get extravagant. Parties and preview events often feature an open bar for several hours following a half-hour presentation; it's social, so it's subtle. Other times it's more tangible: rollerblades to promote an inline skating game. Electric guitars for a music-based title. A BMX bike signed by the game's star athlete. An iPod for a big franchise anniversary. Instances of tchotchkes worth more than 10 bucks are not common and are generally reserved for one person per publication—often the editor-in-chief, because that's the person who has the most editorial power, of course. But hey, pieces of swag worth a few hundred bucks are common enough to rattle off a list of examples from memory, so they're not exactly rare.

"There's a point in time when people get too carried away with tchotchkes," admits Chris Kramer. "But my philosophy is, if you're going to do a tchotchke, do it right. Don't do a cheap piece of crap. Don't do a pen set; don't do a letter opener. Do something that is reflective of the game or brand or company, or something that is going to gain interest and make people think about your game or brand in some sort of way. *EverQuest II*, we made swords. Guess what? It was a fantasy MMO. And we knew those swords were going to live forever, wherever they went—they were going to be mounted on walls, propped up against desks, stuff like that."

Tchotchkes don't need to be physical either; trips are a popular tchotchke, such as taking game editors to a driving school for a day to let them experience auto racing first-hand so they'll be better able to appreciate the realism in a driving game. Other times the link is more tenuous—come to our editor's day, says the company, except it's actually three days, and it's in some sunny exotic locale that has little bearing on any of the titles being shown.

Clearly, this can blow up into a major ethical issue, such as the time that a game based on the seven deadly sins sent out a copy of *Playboy* to signify lust and an actual $50 bill to symbolize greed. Whoa—did you just send an editor cold, hard cash to "promote" your game? At what point are you trying to sway them, to buy their positive opinion?

Many magazines and websites have an internal rule about the value of a gift; if it's below a set number, you can keep it with permission, but if it's more than that, send it back or refuse it outright. This includes trips. If a preview opportunity or the increasingly common review event ("we won't send you the game, but come to us, and we'll let you play the game for 48 hours or more while we put you up in a hotel") has editorial merit but you feel uncomfortable being on their dime, then the game publisher should not pay for your plane ticket—you get your own butt to the destination, or you tell them to just send you the info after the fact.

So is swag evil? Not inherently. "The thought behind it is *not* to influence people to rate your game higher," asserts Schlosberg. "That would be an insult to the journalist." The videogame industry is hardly the inventor of promotional items; they exist more or less everywhere. It's just that it's a younger industry than most, and the people being tempted are generally young as well, so the chance for unethical behavior is higher. And besides, you already get to play games for a living; do you need free gifts to sweeten the deal?

Some years back, one person who came into this industry from a hard news perspective saw tchotchkes as payola, made a huge stink about it, and annoyed a lot of potential freelance employers. However, despite saying how offensive and ethically wrong he felt the swag was, he wouldn't send them back or ask to be removed from the swag list. Publishers will always do that if you just let them know how you feel—it's actually no big deal to say "thanks but no thanks," and several press outlets politely decline any gifts at all. This person, however, actually boasted at the end of one of his columns that he enjoyed the trinkets he'd gotten that week, but he had no idea who sent them or for what game. Maybe his aim was true—"these don't matter, and I'm calling you out on it"—but it sure seemed hypocritical. Plus, he didn't exactly shy away from the media attention given to his own writing and publication as a result of his industry criticism.

Personally, I never felt taking a t-shirt for a game I'd supported was going to send me to editorial hell; I don't subscribe to the idea that you either reject all gifts or you are corrupt. Instead, I believe in trusting your instincts and your own ethical compass. If you get something in the mail that makes you feel compromised, unethical, or otherwise uncomfortable…send it back. It's that simple. If you can accept it with a clear conscience, and your editor and staff feel the same, it's yours. You can give it away to the readers if you like, which is a route many media outlets choose. At the very least, if you do keep cool swag, don't turn right around and sell it on eBay—there's a special level of Hell for people who would do that. And in the meantime, don't open the swag package on video and make fun of it, which I've actually seen some websites do. It makes the reader feel envious, makes the sender feel unappreciated, and cements your reputation as an enormous douchebag.

I believe a tchotchke might buy my attention, but it does not buy my opinion. I believe this because I also believe I am incredibly easy to replace. Whether I'm a freelancer, a full-time staffer, or at the top of someone's editorial food chain, if I let myself be swayed by this stuff, I am out of a job faster than it takes to read this sentence. It's a conscious decision, and it requires some diligence, but my editorial integrity is worth way, way more than a baseball cap, a letter opener, a small toy, and a t-shirt—*combined*. As Chris Kramer puts it, "If I can buy an opinion for the cost of a pen with the game logo on it, I need to start sending out more checks for two dollars for better reviews, because I could just go direct."

It's ultimately a matter of personal moral fiber, which your publication may or may not help you enforce. But if you like your job, don't like tchotchkes more.

WHERE HAVE I READ THAT BEFORE?
How five words that aren't yours can take your career away

Tight deadlines that stack up faster than Tetris blocks can leave you breathless, barely able to think about your current assignment because you're mentally preoccupied with your next one. There have been times I've seen someone's online article or read a press release during research, only to type nearly the same thing without realizing it a few minutes later. Oops—rewrite, stat.

That's the warm fuzzy version of plagiarism, because it was unintentional and caught before it went to print. Knowingly reading someone's review, feature, or interview and cutting and pasting it into your articles is decidedly less heartwarming. And yet, it happens. The motivations are clear: There's polished, concise copy *right there for the taking.* If the writer is talented, maybe you simply can't think of a better way to say it, so to get past writer's block, you "borrow" what their words so you can continue plowing through your assignment. And if the original source is small, like a fan-run website, whose article will get more exposure? Who's gonna know?

These temptations are never, ever to be indulged—this is an ethical line that you should not even be considered as crossable. Never mind the simple selfish fact that you wouldn't want anybody to steal your stuff—consider the repercussions for a second. If you're writing for *Official Game Critics* and it suddenly becomes apparent that large chunks of your latest preview of *Alien Shot III* originally appeared on *Fanworld Central*, you have completely shattered your reputation and quite possibly killed your career for good. Once a thief, always a thief. And that's not even getting into the irreparable harm you just caused the outlet that employs you, which could quite possibly take legal action against you.

Mind you, there are only so many ways to say "fighting game," and inevitably you will, by pure chance, come up with a turn of phrase, a headline, or a joke that someone else has also printed in another publication. If you and another writer and both fishing in a shallow pool of puns, that can be explained away fairly easily. (But next time, go for a less common joke.) It's when the similarities are too obvious to ignore—like when someone changes verbs and adjectives but not sentence structure or opinion—that things get embarrassing and dangerous.

In the mid-'90s, it got downright ugly when print magazines lifted entire FAQs from fans online and printed them wholesale. Sometimes those authors were credited, sometimes those authors were paid…and sometimes neither. That kind of thing is less likely to happen now simply because both sides are aware that it can happen. Pro editors know that everything on the Internet is not free, and many FAQ writers wisely include copyright notices on their work. (Their copyright claim begins when the work is created. So does yours for any writing you publish yourself on a blog or a site you own.) Plus, so many gamers read both pro-based and fan-created content that any suspicious similarities are immediately shouted out in public forums. And it's a good bet that the only time you'll hear noise is when the big guys steal from the little guys, not the other way around—even though that happens sometimes, too.

Still, the burden of not screwing up remains on you. If you're only as good as your last article, you should have enough pride in your work at this point that you would rather rise on the words you put together yourself than sink to the depths of someone else's shadow.

THE CARE AND FEEDING OF YOUR EGO

What if it turns out that you're *not* the reason videogame publications exist?

I touched on ego and the noble reasons for becoming a reviewer earlier in the book, but now that we're into the career-making aspect of it, it bears revisiting. Ego is something that winds up messing up the lives of otherwise great reviewers. In order to put your opinions out there and be willing to defend them, you have to have some confidence. But when that confidence turns into arrogance—and man, can it ever—that's when the problems begin.

Ego's not always easy to keep in check, because the numbers are not in your favor. Take your pride in what you write, add it with the encouragement of friends and family (which proves your instincts) and the positive feedback of readers (which proves you have impact), then multiply by your publication's current circulation/web traffic reports (which proves you have volume). Adjust the results based on how many A-list titles you've reviewed in the last year, and boom! It's easy to let it all go to your head and start thinking that you are super cool and everybody else could learn a thing or two from you if only they'd shut up and listen to your every word. (Please disregard the fact that this sentence could also be used to describe the motivation for writing a book.)

In truth, your job is what's cool. You are afforded incredible opportunities through your work, but if you did not have this job, you wouldn't get to do any of them. Knowing your role and respecting your good fortune are the keys to keeping a level head. Kind words and deeds from PR people are generally offered because that person appreciates what you do for them and their company's products, not because you are a groovy guy who deserves preferential treatment and free goodies. If you start believing your own hype, getting cool opportunities like interviewing your heroes or playing a game months before it's released suddenly go from eye-popping perks or deeply respected honors to grumpy business as usual and cries of "you call that a free t-shirt?" This is the path to the dark side. And once you go there, that haughty attitude starts coloring your reviews, your conversations with friends, your blog entries, everything. You wake up one day, and suddenly you're a jerk.

The best way to avoid an ego explosion is to enlist trusted friends and/or co-workers to tell you that you're a jerk. If you can keep yourself in check without your friends needing to watch you, great; otherwise, expect a sting when they level with you. Of course, you then have to remember that this is a person whose judgment you trust, and you must be willing to ask yourself, honestly, if they're right.

Now, if you do not trust anyone to fulfill this ego-checking duty for you, I suppose I can lower myself to pretending to be one of your "friends" in the meantime. Repeat after me:

I am not a celebrity. I'm a writer.

I am only as good as my last article.

If I become more trouble than I am worth, I can and will be replaced.

I worked hard to get here—but I am lucky to be able to do what I do.

The rules apply to me.

The readers come first.

Now, repeat that once every hour.

Seriously, an ego problem can kill your reputation, both with readers and with your peers. If nobody from either group wants to listen to what you have to say, you're sunk. It can happen to anybody—and the more time you spend in the industry, the more cool stuff you'll experience, and the more likely you are to succumb to entitlement issues, unless you stay actively aware of how you treat people. Some people have this awareness built into their personality naturally and never really have an issue with it on the job. Other people get to the point where they can't stop sounding sarcastically superior and make "tsk" noises when other people do or say something deemed inferior in their presence. (I'm not exaggerating.) Guess which editor is going to last?

Criticizing the Critic

Armchair quarterbacks—gotta love 'em. They're the guys who aren't in the game but can tell you how to play from their perfect view from the couch. Game critics have their own critics in turn…and they often don't seem to have a good perspective on what's going on, either. But that doesn't stop them from pointing out all your flaws!

Hey, fair is fair. You're sitting in judgment of other people's creative works; you don't think you're immune to the same slings and arrows, do you? With or without malice, you've dished it out, so you must be prepared to take it.

Criticism of your work generally comes from three tiers: People who know more than you, people who know the same amount as you, and people who don't know as much as you. To know how to take the criticism, you just have to consider the source. Are you getting something constructive (yet still surprisingly brutal and unflinching) from an informed reader, or are you getting ripped a new one by some jerk who's simply jealous of your job or is pissed off because you didn't parrot his own opinion?

Every time you give a game a bad review, the game's creator is likely thinking the same thing: How much does this guy really know? Was I aware of the flaws? Can I get over how the person expressed their criticism to extract the nuggets of truth? Will this help me do better next time? If you're making them stop and think about what they've done and said, you should stop and think about the same things too.

Taking informed, constructive criticism is the only way to improve. You follow your instincts so often that after a while, the only true insights into your process may come from people completely removed from it. When it comes to criticism, take it for what it's worth, take it to heart, take stock in your methods and performance. Just take it, because it's valuable stuff.

FACTORING IN YOUR FAVORITES

Is there a gentle way to force your personal taste down your audience's throat?

Does this sound familiar? "Those guys at *Official Game Critics* are total morons. Why are they giving all this coverage to *Alien Shot 4* when games like *Happy Fun Obscurity* are being totally ignored? I swear, if I was in charge, things would be totally different."

That might sound familiar because you might have said it. And here you are, years later, having chased your dream and trapped it in a corner. You have something resembling the power of the press, and you can create previews, features, and maybe even event stories based on whatever games seem worthy.

Naturally, the games that are the most worthy are the ones you personally like. As Miyamoto is your witness, an atrocity like the *Happy Fun Obscurity* snubbing will never happen again.

Uh oh. How do you put your personal gaming passions in perspective to what your audience actually, you know, wants?

If you're going to cover niche titles, cover them in a way that shares your passion with everybody else. Writing an all-too-well-versed summary of your favorite small-time game with a hipster tone of voice won't actually unlock its magic for the rest of the world. If you want to keep it as your personal secret passion, then don't complain about it getting snubbed. But if you're ready to trumpet your love to the heavens, make it accessible to everybody so they understand what they're missing and may choose to miss it no longer.

The games you love are often the hardest to write about because you cannot come up with suitable words. You will sound like a fanboy. And just to be clear, that's a bad thing because fanboys lack judgment and objectivity. You are actually being paid to sound like a professional capable of seeing both the good and the bad aspects of any given franchise. A love poem doesn't do that.

The flip side: Let your editors and fellow staff members know what you're crazy about, what you know best, and what you are best suited to write. Many times editors want an "expert" to cover the game going forward. I've covered a lot of skateboarding and music games because I have an affinity for both genres. I have a rep for covering them, like a reporter with a specific beat. It makes sense to play to those strengths. But just because I think they're enjoyable genres doesn't mean that everything I cover about them is deserving of high scores and big features.

This extends to things like the big games getting all the attention from your media outlet. What you love may not sell, and what sells may be in direct opposition to what you like. If the numbers come back that the last *Alien Shot* feature got great feedback or that traffic on the website spiked when the last screenshot collection of *Rock Fight* went online, no amount of championing your favorite franchise will make a difference. The public has spoken…and so has your boss.

You'll quite often need to put your personal loves aside and do what's right for the publication. As long as your employer is cool with it, you can always blog about *Happy Fun Obscurity* on your own time.

HOW IT ALL FALLS APART—AND WHY THAT MIGHT BE GOOD

It may seem painful to abandon this line of work, but what kind of corpse do you want to leave?

You can love something with all your soul, but if you do too much of it, it's only natural that you are going to eventually need a break. So while it may seem impossible that, after all that effort and hard work establishing yourself in the games media, you might want to stop covering videogames. But it's a valid option, and it's one that you probably should take. Someday.

I transitioned into covering videogames from covering music. I was a record reviewer, I interviewed up-and-coming bands, stuff like that. After a few years, I slowly realized...I'm not saying things of value any more. The music I was reviewing—the music I had to cover because it was fresh and new and in stores—was not moving my soul. It was not giving me inspiration enough to talk about it in any meaningful way. I struggled through a few reviews looking for my voice—my valid, insightful, helpful-consumer-advice voice—and simply couldn't find it. I realized it was time to move on. I didn't stop loving music; I stopped loving *covering* music, and it showed. And thankfully, I was the first to realize it. I was happy to return to being a music scholar and music enthusiast and was grateful for my time as a music critic. Since then, writing the occasional record review or article on a band's history has been enough to scratch the itch.

Three or four years later, I found myself with another crisis of conscience. I started to burn out on games, and I felt it. This career can be very draining. I've told you all the scary stories—the long hours, the short deadlines, the constant need to produce the single most compelling thing ever seen on the Internet (within the last 15 minutes). And I found myself at a crossroads: Do I find a way to reinvigorate myself, or do I look for a career change? After about three weeks of soul-searching, I chose the former. I attempted to write in ways I never had, to break the rules I'd been following. It worked, and I've been happy as a writer ever since.

Some of my peers have not been so lucky to recognize that moment in their own lives. They are proud to do what they do; they have worked incredibly hard to get there. They refuse to let go because they feel it's all they have. But the fire is gone; they aren't challenged in a healthy positive way and instead find themselves annoyed and jaded. Well, *they* don't find themselves that way—that's the point. Everyone around them looks at them and knows they're not the writer they used to be, and nobody wants to tell them. (And for what it's worth, I've seen this happen to not just writers and editors but entire publications. They keep going on the same uninspired path, long having forgotten where they are headed.)

So just as you took the responsibility to get this career, it falls to you to consider the right time to let it go. Take your vacation time to clear your head; that's why they give it to you. They know you need it. But if you're still unhappy after you've taken a break, be honest with yourself; be self-critical. Are you doing your best work? If not, why not? What is stopping you from it? Are the problems fixable, or have you just fallen out of love with the work? Because if that's the case, that doesn't mean you don't love games; it just means that your time to speak about them and help other people may have come to a close. The work you leave behind will speak for itself. But there are too many people who respect and rely on what you say to keep chugging away as a matter of habit. You're not doing the audience any good, you're not doing your editor any good, and you're certainly not doing your reputation any good. It's better to be remembered as a quality writer than currently known as a once-great writer.

When it's your time to go, leave.

How Not to Burn Out

When you reach your crisis of conscience, nobody will be there to help you. You'll just wake up one day, realize that the source of your dissatisfaction is your own writing output, and get this horrible feeling in the pit of your stomach. Now what?

Nine times out of 10, you can turn it around with a creative challenge. Better still, you can keep that horrible moment out of your life altogether if you simply remain proactive.

There is no one way to do something, least of all when it comes to expressing personal opinion. Look at what works for other people and use it in your own expression. Some people write; others podcast, blog, shoot videos, make animations, whatever. Some people do all that stuff. Try one. Insert a new method into your coverage practices. If you are uninspired by written reviews, try recording one as a podcast. Prepare one review a day for two weeks and see if it suits you. Incorporating new techniques can offer the right spark to reignite your creative fires.

There are also times when you can dig yourself your own rut and not realize you're doing it. The gaming industry you cover will change, sometimes quickly and violently; the media industry you work in will change on its own sympathetic path. It's foolish to think that how you do what you do today will be the same tomorrow, so you should be ready to adapt your methods to fit the times, if not actually seek out those new methods as they emerge. You might self-identify as a blogger or a magazine writer or a podcaster, but suddenly some new form of communication might evolve (really, who saw Twitter coming?), and your editor suddenly informs you that it's part of your job. Don't resist the challenge, don't say you're too busy, don't dig in your heels and insist that "that's not part of my job." Accept it and adapt to it.

Nobody wants to be seen as inflexible, but a nimble writer who really thinks creatively in all aspects of their career is the one who will remain valuable.

GAME OVER. NOW WHAT?

When the game reviews end, another career might begin

One day, you will find yourself out of work. Your site shuts down; you wind up being laid off as part of a restructuring effort; your new startup project didn't start up. You move to a new state or country and can't keep the old job. Or maybe you committed any of the egregious editorial sins I've just discussed and got yourself canned. (You'd better not. I'll disown you.) There are all kinds of ways to stop writing about games, but many of them also open new career doors and offer the potential to stay involved in the same world. Some are more immediately obvious than others.

Custom publishing

Would you like your own magazine? Custom publishing is how you get one. Granted, this helps if you are already in possession of a) a lot of money and b) something that is worth its own magazine. I was the editor of *World of Warcraft: Official Magazine* during its startup period, and that was a custom publication—Future pitched Blizzard on the virtues of having their own magazine, and Blizzard agreed. Similarly, NVidia sponsored *NVision* magazine, and Best Buy has *@Gamer*. These magazines are all staffed by industry vets; they've written for lots of other publications, but these projects give them the opportunity to run their own ship. Some of these mags only last a few issues (*SOE Worlds*, sponsored by Sony Online Entertainment to discuss games like *EverQuest*, *Star Wars Galaxies*, and *PlanetSide*, lasted exactly one issue—but as the executive editor, I will say it was a darned good issue) and some go on for epically long runs. This is basically how *Nintendo Power* got its start, though it eventually evolved into a traditional licensed magazine.

Sometimes there's an interesting trade-off with these projects; because a client like a retailer or a game publisher is footing the bill, you might not have full editorial control—if Blizzard doesn't want you talking about some controversial aspect of *WoW*, for instance, then you don't get to talk about it. Other clients might want exactly what you want to make for them; it's likely to be different every time.

Other forms of custom publishing include more traditional marketing materials and retailer brochures—for instance, those slick glossy booklets that retail stores received a few months before the Xbox 360 came out were products of custom publishing. And of course, there are always new CP ideas being brainstormed, so if you like seeing new forms of gamer communication, working in custom publishing can be very rewarding. The best part: If the biz guys know what they are doing, it can be lucrative too, whether freelance, contract, or full-time.

Consulting

Picture writing an in-depth review of a game before the game is done—several months before it even comes out—and giving that review directly to the publisher. That's what a consultant does. Many publishers hire ex-game reviewers to take a hard, critical look at games in development so the flaws can be identified and fixed before the game hits retail shelves. The reports consultants generate are often targeted and very detailed; it's not uncommon to get a list of questions from the developer or publisher along with a build of the game and a non-disclosure agreement. Consultants generally set their own prices, and it is a competitive market because it's full of veterans with a lot of editorial credibility and a deep understanding of the game-making process, not to mention a healthy collection of industry contacts. But at the same time, publishers will often use several consultants—sometimes due to personal expertise, sometimes just because they want multiple opinions. It's a popular choice among writers who want to set their own deadlines and run their own business.

Columnist

Reviews are one thing; writing a column is a different discipline altogether. It's more personal, definitely opinionated, and potentially inflammatory. It can also be a distinctive offering for a site or publication, something that it can bank on for repeat traffic and building their reputation (as well as further establishing yours). This work is a bit harder to come by, as columnists are generally people with years of experience in their field and a distinct personal voice. Plus, there are only so many slots available in so many publications. Still, it can't hurt to pitch yourself for one; just have six to 12 topics ready before you do.

Quality assurance

As a reviewer, you have spent all your time identifying problems with games and documenting them for all the world to see. What better path for you than quality assurance? Commonly referred to as "the mailroom of the game industry," QA's methodical bug-tracking is not glamorous, but it's utterly crucial. Everything from missing textures to flaky online play must be identified, quantified, and reportified to the development team so they can find and remedy them. The good news: Many people up the food chain in game development got their start in QA, so if you really want to put all that expertise to use and build toward a career in game design (David Jaffe paid his QA dues, among many other notable names), this is worth a look, even if it does mean restarting your career at the ground level. One day, your creative decisions will inspire someone to identify the problems in the games you've created and document them for the world to see!

Game producer

Let's assume that if you had any real skill in math or programming, you'd be building games, not writing about them. For most people, diving in and writing code is not a second career option. But if you have learned how to organize your time, work with a team, and hit deadlines, then serving as an associate producer on a game in development might be a good fit. Producers act as a liaison between the developer and the publisher, making sure that all the team's hard work serves the greater good. They juggle budgets, they keep people informed, they herd cats. Justin Lambros, who spent two years as an associate editor at *GamePro* before moving on to producing gigs at LucasArts, Electronic Arts, and Sega, describes his job as "a daily routine of Sophie's Choices and Murphy's Law. You don't ever want to kill a feature or work that someone does, but whatever can go wrong usually does during a development cycle, and you have to help the team get through it."

And while it's easy to determine what a senior art lead or level designer does on a team, the producer's role is more fluid and less well-defined. "Production is a 'soft skill'—communication, organization, getting things done, and solving problems," says Justin. "It's part salesman, part businessman, and part manager. But at the end of the day, you are relied upon for the on-time, on-budget, high-quality game that was greenlit by your company. You put a team together, enforce milestones, work to keep team morale high, help the marketing team sell the game, and go through every build and every bug in the database with a fine-tooth comb to deliver the best product you can."

Justin notes that producers can come from very different backgrounds, ranging from QA to marketing to artists to even lowly game reviewers—but it's all in how you apply whatever skills you bring to the job and how you grow from there. "Living and breathing videogames over the years that I worked at *GamePro* were great preparation for getting into development," he says. "I got to see what games looked like in development, how games become great, how some things can go wrong. Communication is a key to production, and I saw that first-hand as a journalist. No matter what discipline you work in, the key to be a successful team lead is that you have to be a great communicator. Whether you're telling the team about a design feature, spelling out the visual direction of the art, or troubleshooting a buggy tech feature, you need to be able to express yourself both verbally and also very importantly, in writing. Teams are getting bigger and using a variety of contractors from around the world. You need to be able to communicate about the game you are working on to make sure it comes out well."

Game writer

Well, this one's the dream, isn't it? You already know how to work with words; you have already seen your share of inspired and dismal narratives, in equal measure. And you just happen to have an awesome idea involving space marines that has never been done before. You can do this, right? Maybe. Can you talk to more than just the characters in your head? "Writers at BioWare work very closely with level design, art, and cinematics throughout the process, and often the writer becomes the facilitator among those groups," explains Jay Turner, another *GamePro* alumnus who helped edit *Jade Empire* before writing for *Dragon Age*, *Sonic Chronicles*, and *Mass Effect* 2 and its downloadable add-on content. "On small team projects, I sometimes wind up giving opinions and suggestions on how a level could be more fun, or how to bring a level into consistency with the other levels we're working on. On the core *Mass Effect* team, writers are more specialized, but on the much smaller DLC team, I find that a writer has to understand game-design theory and what makes a game fun—even if that means sacrificing plot moments or cool lines of dialogue so the player can have a great time."

As with a magazine or website staff, your words as a game writer may be your own, but you need to be ready for critical feedback and adapt to group decisions. "While writing is generally a solitary job, your results go into a committee and come out the other end," explains Jay. "There are usually between four and eight writers, plus a lead writer, a lead designer, the lead cinematic designer, art, animation, and the executive producer, all involved in making the game as awesome as they can, but they're talented people who've worked on high-rated, strong-selling games in the past, so that's not always so bad."

But what about that swear-on-my-life-never-been-done-before

space marines concept? When do I get to present my brilliant idea? "You can say, 'Here's my brilliant idea,' but you have to be prepared for the fact that what you wind up with is likely to look nothing like what you walked in with," says Jay. "For instance, Zaeed's Loyalty mission in *ME2* wound up quite different from what I originally proposed. Much of the time, the changes make everything better or cover for some possibility you hadn't considered—like, 'We don't have art for a white space-whale, so your "Space Moby-Dick" story can't work.'"

"As a writer rises in the ranks, the job becomes more organizational," says Jay. "You're not the official manager of the team you're working with, but you have a more outside perspective and have to hold vision over the plot of the entire package. For Zaeed, we had two level designers and maybe three cinematic designers...and one writer for the whole thing. When you're not busy writing, you're busy fielding questions and facilitating communication among the team members."

Realistically, then, writing about games and writing actual games have several things in common—teamwork, diplomacy, putting the material before your ego, and deep insight on the audience. "Editorial gave me an opportunity to really, really know games," admits Jay. "Right now, my knowledge of what gamers like and what they'll put up with, as well as my ability to communicate what I like and don't like and why, are serving me almost as well as any writing ability I might have. The ability to communicate clearly and politically with all sorts of people is invaluable, and that's definitely something I learned in editorial by dealing with PR contacts, developers, and other journalists."

Maybe most importantly, reviewers-turned-writers have a deep understanding of what the press is likely to think. "Editorial gave me perspective that developers don't have," says Jay. "Anytime we're getting all prideful about something in one of our games, I can stand back and go, 'There's probably six other teams doing this exact same thing and 20 journalists ready to roll their eyes and politely say, "Uh huh, yeah, that's great!"'"

Public relations

If the press is assumed to be the free and honest voice of the people, public relations is assumed to be its evil twin. PR departments are in charge of any statements a company makes about its games; as already discussed, they are the people who get the press what they need to do their jobs. On a core level, there are key similarities between the two disciplines—both require strong communication skills, and both deliver a message designed to inform and persuade. (Is there a huge difference between "buy this game because I played it and I think you'll enjoy it" and "buy this game because we made it and we think you'll enjoy it"?) Both, too, require strict adherence to schedules that determine when information reaches the target audience, whether that be creating deadline embargoes or respecting them. As a result, you will sometimes see media types jump the fence to PR (sometimes jokingly called "the dark side") and be quite happy there.

Remember Matt Schlosberg and Abby Oliva from earlier in the book? They both studied journalism in college but made their careers in PR. After leaving *GamePro*, Jay Turner worked as a PR asset coordinator (read: screenshot wrangler) at EA for several months before moving back to editorial. "I also wrote press releases, which I actually kinda enjoyed," he says. "It was frightening how similar writing PR releases was to writing editorial previews, and it made me feel kinda dirty when I went back to writing previews that were more or less regurgitated press releases. But when I did go back, PR folks were a lot more honest with me when they knew

I had been one of them. Their job performance depends on free-range gaming nerds giving them pages in the magazine or on the website. I had one PR rep call me and tell me that he'd get fired if I couldn't get his game into my section of the magazine. I put it in because there wasn't anything better for that 1/3 page, but that's how cutthroat it can be, especially if the company you're working for isn't making games that sell a billion copies or that review in the high 80s or higher every time."

Chris Kramer also wrote for multiple editorial outlets before going into PR, so he knew what mistakes not to make at the get-go. "Nothing was more infuriating on the media side than when someone never got back to me," he says. "The job of PR person is to represent their company, to the public, to the media. If you're not responding to the media, you're not doing your job."

And because he was an editor himself, he has high standards for the writers he works with. "I'm harder on journalists I know who are good writers who aren't taking the time when they're doing their reviews," he admits. "There's a writer that I'm pretty good friends with who I respect a lot and like a lot; he writes for a lot of places, and I think he's a good reviewer. He wrote a really lame review of *Street Fighter IV*, in my opinion; it came down to, 'I don't know, I don't really like *Street Fighter*, and this is kind of the same game, so I don't really get it. If you like it, you'll like it; but if not, you won't, B minus.' And that review fed into Metacritic, and I gave that writer a hard time. And later he was like, 'Are we okay, are we fighting?' I said, 'No, you did your job, I did my job. You wrote a lousy review of my game, and I told you that you wrote a lousy review of my game.'"

Most public relations professionals have excellent people skills, a finely honed ability to multitask, no qualms about solving problems as they appear, and more than anything, incredible patience. If those sound like interesting challenges, go for it.

Community management

Community management is technically an extension of public relations because you are relating to the public, but instead of doing it on a scale of millions, you're doing it one to one. A CM maintains a public presence for a game publisher or game studio while cultivating personal relationships with gamers; they have to be honest *and* on message. It's sometimes tricky, especially when they are held accountable for their company's less popular decisions. You need a thick skin, but you still have to be able to connect with people.

Increasingly popular at both the development and publishing levels, CMs hang out where the customers are (Twitter, Facebook, and forums, among other places), talking with them and getting unvarnished feedback, as well as acting as a face and/or target, so people know who to contact when they have a question or idea. If you enjoyed responding to your publication's emails and liked jumping into comment conversations as a member of a press outlet, this hybrid position of speaking in an editorial manner on a company's behalf might be a good fit. Jeff Green, editor-in-chief of *Computer Gaming World* in the past and PopCap's director of editorial and social media in the present, simply called this weird mix of duties and loyalties "not journalism." I haven't found a better term.

Point being, you can still be surrounded by the industry you love even if you no longer have a job at a pure editorial outlet. You can keep your distance and observe from a new perspective, or you can try to actually participate in the business you've been covering for all this time. You're guaranteed to learn something, no matter what.

Write a book about how to be a game reviewer

Meh. It's been done.

■BONUS LEVEL■
100% It

There's always something more you can do to prepare yourself for the next hurdle. Tackle these extra challenges and see if they make you a better writer than you already are.

RANDOM INSTANCES FOR XP

How do you get to *Official Game Critics*? Practice.

At this point, you may be suffering from information overload and not really know where to start. Start with some of these exercises, which should help you start to find your voice, face some challenges, and start honing your chops. Give yourself 100 XP for each one you successfully complete. Then give yourself a cookie.

• Write a complete review that does not exceed 50 words.

• Take someone else's review and edit it down to 100 words.

• Play a game and then write a negative review of it. Then write the positive one.

- Write the same a review twice—once using first-person voice, once without.

- Generate five headlines that might accompany a feature-length story preview of the last game you played.

- Come up with a 200-word sidebar that would accompany that feature-length review.

- Figure out what is interesting enough about that game that deserves its own standalone explanation

- Take five screens of a PC game. Write captions for them to explain why they are contextually important to your review.

- Write a review without using the words "graphics," "sound" or "controls"—and without using analog words like "visuals" or "audio."

- Have a friend buy you a magazine and tear off the cover before giving it to you. Read the mag, then write the coverlines. Then get your cover back and compare your ideas to what the editors did.

- Write up five detailed feature pitches for your favorite mag. Include art and layout concepts for each one.

- Who's your favorite game developer? Whose work doesn't impress you? Now come up with 10 original, creative interview questions for each.

RECOMMENDED READING

If you have enjoyed this book,
why not read another?

I'm betting you already have several gaming websites bookmarked and you read reviews, news, and other articles there on a regular (if not hourly) basis. And why not? It's free, it's frequent, and it beats working or studying. But since you already know how to read, there are a few other things out there I'd recommend you seek out and devour as you get more serious about this career.

There are many books about videogames, but if I had to pick the three most useful and interesting ones, it would be these:

Game Over: Press Start to Continue
By David Sheff with new chapters by Andy Eddy
ISBN 0966961706
This is the latest printing from 1999 (the original 1993 edition is ominously titled *Game Over: How Nintendo Zapped an American*

Industry, Captured Your Dollars, and Enslaved Your Children) and, while currently out of print, the updated edition will be easier to find and has more interviews anyway. Sheff is no friend to gaming, but that skeptical attitude serves this book well—a fascinating history of Nintendo with all the juicy gossip you'd care to read. Even if you aren't a fan of Nintendo or its products, its market-defining rise to power is a fascinating story. The chapter on *Tetris* alone reads with all the excitement of a spy thriller. And while you're absorbing the content, don't ignore the presentation; *Game Over* is an excellent lesson in how to find the human angles of the business aspects of the game industry. Andy Eddy's chapters fill in some crucial historical periods, including the launch of the Nintendo 64.

The Ultimate History of Video Games: From Pong to Pokémon—
The Story Behind the Craze That Touched Our Lives and Changed
the World
By Steven Kent
ISBN 0761536434
I've always felt this book lived up to its name. It's the most conversational yet comprehensive history of the game industry I've read, from the earliest days of Atari and Magnavox through to the modern era. It's packed with insightful, compelling quotes from Kent's extensive interviews with the people who made the history. Because it covers the first 25 years of the industry, it was originally published under the name *The First Quarter*, but *Ultimate* is what you'll find in print today.

Trigger Happy: Videogames and the Entertainment Revolution
By Stephen Poole
ISBN 1559705396
Stephen Poole is a long-time columnist for well-respected U.K.

gaming culture magazine *Edge,* and this book analyzes what makes games uniquely games—aesthetically, compared to other forms of art and entertainment. I loved the book (I read the U.S. edition published in 2004); when I read it, it made me consider games from a different perspective. Best of all, Poole has now made the book available for free download as a PDF under the Creative Commons license. You can download it from http://stevenpoole.net/blog/trigger-happier/

Of course, there's plenty to read beyond books:

As many gaming websites as you can stand

The problem with the Internet is that it never ends. You can't read all the game coverage that appears on it. Pick several, load up your RSS reader, and start studying how the different sites cover the same stories. Look for tone of voice, word choice, the sense of humor (and whether it swings silly or cruel), length of articles, and the ratio of news to opinion. Every one will likely be different.

Every game magazine you can get your hands on

"Every" is a lot easier now than it was, because sadly, there aren't nearly as many as there once were. Subscribe to at least one, and grab others at the newsstand. As with websites, it's worth seeing how competing mags do the same thing in different ways—look for all of the above editorial approaches in print as well. And if you can find it, I also recommend *Game Developer* magazine, because it shows me a side of the industry that I can always learn more about.

Every non-game publication you can get your hands on

The term "craft" is used a lot when it comes to writing because it's more than just words on a paper; it's how they're put together with

the images on the page, how the space on every page is used—
there's a level of aesthetics that comes into play. Widening your
focus so you're not just looking at gaming publications is amazingly
valuable—pick up lots of different magazines, from fashion to gossip
to lifestyle to technical, and check out blogs on dedicated topics
beyond gaming. The closest cousins will like be "passion hobby"
magazines—titles that cover one narrow topic and go deep, the way
most game enthusiast magazines cover games. Car magazines are
always a good example of this, but you have plenty of options.

Any and all mainstream game coverage

When *Time* does a cover story about videogaming, read it. When
your local paper talks about the holiday rush for this year's hot
system, read it. It's crucial to step away of the "enthusiast press" and
see what everybody else is saying about gaming. You are a gamer;
you follow your hobby very closely. The average local daily, where
the writer may also have several other entertainment beats to cover,
maybe not so much. It's always educational to see how non-gaming
publications cover gaming. And hey, if you don't like what you find,
maybe there's a job opportunity in there for you.

Send in the Blogs

I'm not recommending any specific blogs in this reading list.
That's not because I don't think that there are any good ones to
read—kind of the opposite. But the text in the publications above
is edited; there was at least one editor reading the author's work
before it went out the door, and likely, several people contributed
to polishing the text. The result is (usually) text that you can safely
use as a template for your own.

Meanwhile, blog posts trade on their immediacy, so the
mechanics are not always right; you're really left up to the writer's

own diligence when it comes to whether or not any given blog is a good example to follow. So by all means, read them—read them all, if you have that much time. But be aware that you may be digesting the raw feed instead of the refined signal.

ACKNOWLEDGEMENTS

Thanks.

I've written this slowly over a period of several years—partly to consider the advice I was giving and make sure it would last the test of time, and partly because playing games is still more fun than writing about them and takes far less discipline.

If you're not one of the people listed here, I don't expect you to read this page. But if you choose to read it anyway and you run into one of these people, now you'll have something to talk about. I want to offer some sincere thanks, because this book wouldn't have happened without them.

My parents Richard and Delores Amrich for encouraging both my gaming and writing, for instilling my work ethic as well as my life ethics, and for always letting me have a quarter when we passed an arcade;

Barbara Adams, whose Ithaca College course Writing as a Critic showed me my hidden talents, and whose subsequent relentless encouragement helped kick-start my entire career;

Brad Tolinski, who gave me my first shot in part because I was weird and insistent; and Harold Steinblatt, who was patient with me on my first editing job when he totally had no reason to be;

Jeff Kitts, who showed me how everything worked, and who is still, unfortunately, the deathmatch champion;

My brother-from-another-mother Andy Eddy, who literally gave me food and shelter when I took the biggest risk of my life, and opened innumerable industry doors for me as a mentor;

Wes Nihei, Eric Bratcher, and Francesca Reyes, who all provided the blueprint for what an editor-in-chief should be—creative but clear, open-minded but decisive, and most of all, calm in a storm of deadline-fueled chaos;

Frank Parisi, who got me thinking about codifying my little office rants into a structured format;

Paul Curthoys, who has been the supportive and encouraging little editor on my shoulder for a long time—my go-to reality check on most things I've written in the last 15 years, including this book;

Pete Babb, the head buckaroo of the Grammar Rodeo, who worked with me at *GamePro* and was therefore the perfect choice to copy-edit this sucker;

Matt Schlosberg, Lisa Fields, Chris Kramer, Robert Taylor, Abby Oliva, Rob Smith, Sid Shuman, Jay Turner, Justin Lambros, Corey Cohen, Mitchell Dyer, Justin McElroy, Marc Saltzman, Ken Rosman, Sarita Churchill, Ryan Jones, AJ Glasser, Gabe Graziani, Logan Decker, and Cameron Lewis for their time, wisdom, suggestions, support, and patience in filling in gaps in my knowledge;

Cliff Bleszinski and Dana Cowley, for the fantastic foreword, massive help, and kind permissions;

And last but absolutely not least, Katrin Auch, who not only laid out the book, designed the cover, and built the website, but is the reason for all of this—the book, the career, getting up in the morning, everything. *Sa saol seo agus an chéad cheann eile.*

ABOUT THE AUTHOR

Dan Amrich started reviewing videogames professionally in 1993, when Super NES and Sega Genesis ruled the earth. Over the 15 years that followed, he served as Senior Editor for *Official Xbox Magazine*, GamesRadar, and *GamePro*; Executive Editor of *GameSport* and *Digital Diner*; and Editor-in-Chief of *World of Warcraft: Official Magazine*. He has written freelance articles for national publications including *Wired, PC Gamer, Blender, Slam, Guitar World,* and *Time Out New York,* and he is the author of the 2006 book *PlayStation 2 for Dummies.*

Dan is currently trapped in Los Angeles with his lovely wife Katrin, three cats, a couple of arcade machines, and more guitars than anyone should own. You can contact him directly at dan@criticalpathbook.com or @DanAmrich on Twitter, but he won't give you a job.

Made in the USA
Lexington, KY
22 November 2013